T0149506

Packing Light

For the Journey of Motherhood

LAURA ELLIS

ONE MOM'S TESTIMONY OF BEING SET FREE
FROM THE PRISON OF LEGALISM

WESTBOW
PRESS®
A DIVISION OF THOMAS NELSON
& ZONDERVAN

Some content taken from TRANSFORMING GRACE, by Jerry Bridges.
Copyright © 1991, 2008. Used by permission of NavPress. All rights
reserved. Represented by Tyndale House Publishers, Inc

WestBow Press books may be ordered through booksellers or by contacting:

WestBow Press
A Division of Thomas Nelson & Zondervan
1663 Liberty Drive
Bloomington, IN 47403
www.westbowpress.com
1 (866) 928-1240

Scripture quotations are from the ESV® Bible (The Holy Bible, English
Standard Version®), copyright © 2001 by Crossway, a publishing ministry
of Good News Publishers. Used by permission. All rights reserved.

ISBN: 978-1-5127-7751-2 (sc)
ISBN: 978-1-5127-7752-9 (hc)
ISBN: 978-1-5127-7750-5 (e)

Library of Congress Control Number: 2017902973

Print information available on the last page.

WestBow Press rev. date: 03/30/2019

To my husband, Mickey:
this book is really yours—
minus twenty thousand words or so
(and the excessive use of parentheses
and exclamation points, of course!)

Thank you
for consistently pointing me
to Jesus.

And for my seven little *(and not so little)* blessings:
Elijah
Esther
Eva
Ezekiel (Zeke)
Eden
Elizabeth (Lulu)
& Ezra

It is the cry of my heart
that you choose to follow the Shepherd
all the days of your lives.

CONTENTS

Introduction... ix

Chapter 1   Grey Is *Not* the New Black......................... 1

Chapter 2   Gently Led to Gently Lead 13

Chapter 3   Love Is the Goal 27

Chapter 4   Different by Design 39

Chapter 5   Shadow of the Supermom 53

Chapter 6   When God Guides, He Provides................ 63

Chapter 7   Free to Be Me!............................... 75

Chapter 8   Making Peace with Ramen Noodles............. 79

Chapter 9   The Homemaking Balance.................... 95

Chapter 10   Finding My Own Version of Beautiful 111

Chapter 11   Navigating the Sea of Choices................. 125

Chapter 12   "Matchmaker, Matchmaker, Make Me a Match"... 137

Chapter 13   A Spacious Place............................. 151

Appendix A   The Gospel of Jesus Christ 163

Appendix B   A Great Way to Do Devotions................. 169

Appendix C   Scripture Songs 173

Acknowledgments.. 177

INTRODUCTION

**I apologized to Elijah (6) for being so grouchy one day.
He whispered in my ear,
"Take it to the bottom of the ocean."
At my look of surprise, he then explained,
"When you tell God you are sorry,
He will throw your sins to the bottom of the ocean."**

**You will cast all our sins
into the depths of the sea.**
–Micah 7:19

Whenever I read a book, I always want to know right away about the author, so I'd like to start by sharing some things about myself: First and foremost, I am loved and redeemed by the Savior of the world—*nothing else even comes close to that kind of amazing!* He is my "exceedingly great reward" (Genesis 15:1 NKJV), and my life is a testament to His amazing grace. I'm married to a very patient man (as in, "longsuffering," because the poor man has suffered *long*). And I am also a perpetually-clad-in-dark-stretchy-pants mother of seven children, which means I have changed approximately 38,325 diapers. (I did the math and that number is on the conservative end!) I've been carrying around babies for so long that sometimes when I go shopping, I find myself bouncing whatever is in my arms. Like a paper towel holder. Yes, I did. Once, I even dropped a glass in the sink while washing dishes and actually started to *comfort it!* (Yeah, I didn't get out much for quite awhile . . .)

I am so not "Mom of the Year" material. In fact, I major in meltdowns (not talking about my toddlers here), and have had to apologize to my kids more times than I care to admit. Parenting has often been for me what I like to refer to as a "gauntlet of sanctification." But even though I have often struggled in this calling, I can say from the bottom of my heart that I am *so very blessed* to be a mama.

---

*Eva (3) asked, "When am I going to be a mommy?" "Not for a while," I told her. She was definitely *not* happy about that, complaining that it was "taking *sooooooo* long!"

*Lulu (6) was playing that she was a mom and Ezra (4) was her child. He wasn't listening very well, and I overheard her lamenting to him that "it is *so hard* to be a mother!"

As I began my second decade of parenting, I realized the sweet older ladies in the grocery store were right—it does go by fast! (It is equally true, as my friend Page says, that though the years fly by, some days are *long*—like those I-am-pretty-sure-an-entire-week-just-passed-by-and-it-isn't-even-naptime-yet kind of days.) When the younger generation of women in my church started having babies, I realized I am no longer one of the young moms on campus. It was also surprising when a couple new mamas started asking me for advice. Me? The woman who still doesn't know how to potty-train, can find herself arguing with preschoolers, and *for the love of everything* can't figure out how to get her children to use less bath towels each week?

I may not have much to offer in the way of practical child-training advice, but I do have something heavy on my heart to share with other moms—be a Berean (Acts 17:11), and check everything you read and hear against the plumb line of God's Word. This message was stamped on my heart, so to speak, through some hard trials in my early mothering, and this book tells that story.

My *one* potty-training tip—When kids start using sarcasm, they are most likely capable of going to the bathroom by themselves:

I was putting Elijah (3) into his car seat and smelled something. I told him, "Something stinks!" and asked if he had a dirty diaper. He looked at me and said, "Maybe *you* stink, Mom."

Disclaimers and Such

- I tried to be real in this book, but when I read it, it just seems like a better me and cheerier home life is being presented. And since I don't want to add several chapters detailing all of my sins and struggles (because who wants to read that?), I'm going to have to ask you to think of this book like a Christmas card photo: this *is* what my life looks like, it just isn't the whole picture. (When we are tempted to compare our lives with the limited knowledge we have about someone else's, we need to remember that Sunday mornings, blog posts, and books are only pieces of a person's reality. No one's life is free of difficulty, and all of us are works-in-progress in this Christian life, to one degree or another.)
- I have not read all of the books I quoted from, so the citations are not endorsements (unless a recommendation is also given).
- If you wonder why the pronouns for God are sometimes capitalized and sometimes not, it is because most of the Bible versions I used don't capitalize them while I prefer to do so.
- This isn't exactly a light topic, so to add some humor to these pages, I've included a bunch of quotes from my kids and several other children. For the times they were almost a certain age, like "six and three quarters," or I hadn't recorded how old they were when they said something, I have given an approximate age, which is noted by the following symbol: ~

In my Sunday School class, Jayden (4) asked Jubilee (6) if she lived in California. She said she did, and with much excitement he said, "Wow! You live *right next* to me!"

- If you are like me and frequently jump ahead when reading, *I encourage you not to,* because the first part of this book is foundational to the rest of it.
- I write about my personal experiences a lot in this book because they help to illustrate my message, but I never want that, or my zeal to expose legalism, to take away from the main thing, which is Jesus: Colossians 1:28 says, *"Him we proclaim,* warning everyone and teaching everyone with all wisdom, that we may present everyone mature in Christ" (emphasis mine). It is always ultimately about our King of Glory and His glorious Gospel. May not one word in these pages detract from that truth!
- I also need to clarify what is meant by the words "Being Set Free from the Prison of Legalism" on the cover of this book. What I am referring to with the word "being" is "continuing to be." While the Lord has done an amazing work of freeing me from much legalism, the truth is, it is still a battle of needing to take legalistic thoughts captive and make them obedient to Christ (2 Corinthians 10:5). In fact, I believe one of the reasons God had me write this book was so that I could read it!
- Lastly, it is extremely important to note that I am writing to a Christian audience. If you do not have saving faith in Christ, I urge you to read Appendix A, as it is the most important message you will *ever* hear about the most important decision you will *ever* have to make.

Mica Campbell wrote the following: "When we are willing to give King Jesus our mess, He turns it into our message."[1] I am incredibly humbled and immeasurably blessed that God has taken my mess and, through it, given me a message to share. May we know the truth and be set free (John 8:32)!

The following line from the Jars of Clay song "Love Song for a Savior" has long reminded me of freedom from legalism (it also inspired the cover of this book):

In open fields of wildflowers,
she breathes the air and flies away[2]

(emphasis mine)

---

[1] Campbell, Micca. "When Your Mess Becomes Your Message," accessed June 29, 2017, http://proverbs31.org/devotions/devo/when-your-mess-becomes-yourmessage-2/.
[2] Haseltine, Dan, Matthew Ryan Bronleewe, Charlie Lowell, and Stephen Daniel Mason. *Jars of Clay*. CD. Franklin: Essential Records, 1995.

Eva Ellis

CHAPTER I
Grey Is *Not* the New Black

I realized I might need to add a little color to my wardrobe
when Eva (~ 3) said something to me along the lines of
"You know when I'm a mom and wear black . . ."
She said it so matter-of-factly— doctors wear white,
mechanics wear grey, and moms wear, you know, black.

During my first pregnancy, a friend gave me a book that said scheduled feeding and sleeping is *the* Biblical way to care for an infant. The authors misused Scripture at times to substantiate their opinions, and gave extreme fictional examples of children not parented according to their parenting philosophy. I certainly did not want to raise the kind of tyrannical child they portrayed! And, of course, I wanted to parent according to God's will, but it didn't take long for me to begin to realize that this method was not for us. (Please know, I am not saying it is wrong universally—just that it has not been right for our individual family . . . yet. I know the Lord could lead us differently in the future.)

While I personally didn't feel comfortable parenting according to what was put forth in the book, it was still a struggle for me to shake the things I had read in there. Had I really chosen an unbiblical way to mother my little ones? (And how my deeply rooted pride hated the thought that others might think so, but that is a topic for another book!) This was a time of extreme confusion and emotional turmoil for me. On one hand, my husband, Mickey, (and I, at times) had a peace about the way we were caring for our babies. On the other hand, I was often conflicted when I heard other mothers talk about baby scheduling, because I assumed they were speaking in the context of it being God's universal will. Again, the fear would creep in that I was parenting contrary to His will and harming my children.

I now know that scheduled infant feeding and sleeping is not *the way* to care for a baby — it is *a* way. Of course, there are many things that are *the way* God wants us to do something. They are sometimes referred to as the Black and Whites of Scripture, which are the clear teachings and universal commands of God contained in the Bible. If He says it, so should we! Or as my dad said, "If the Bible says 'do,' we do; if the Bible says 'don't,' we don't." (Old Testament law is to be understood in light of New Testament teaching. More on this later.) Then there are Grey areas, like infant care, which are issues in life that the Bible does not address. If He doesn't say it, we shouldn't either! By that, I mean we should never uphold standards of righteousness that He has not made. To do so, is to fall into legalism. Colossians 2:8 says, "See to it that no one takes you captive by philosophy and empty deceit, according to human tradition, according to the elemental spirits of the world, and not according to Christ."

Some Black and Whites:

In Galatians 5:19–21, we are told that "the works of the flesh *are evident*: sexual immorality, impurity, sensuality, idolatry, sorcery, enmity, strife, jealousy, fits of anger, rivalries, dissensions, divisions, envy, drunkenness, orgies, and things like these" (emphasis mine).

"But the fruit of the Spirit is love, joy, peace, patience, kindness, goodness, faithfulness, gentleness, self-control; against such things there is no law" (Galatians 5:22, 23).

Admittedly, there may be some Black and Whites in Scripture that are not immediately understandable to everyone. When in doubt, we should always ask the Lord for clarity. Jesus said the Spirit came to guide us into all truth (John 16:13), and we can trust Him to show us what we need to know.

Making into Law the Traditions of Men

A misunderstanding of the difference between the Black and Whites and Grey areas is the cause for many divisive issues within the church today. Whole ministries have even been built upon the assertion that their particular methods or teachings regarding Grey areas are *the* Biblical way. Examples of Grey areas that are commonly addressed in a legalistic manner are: the particulars regarding modesty, educational choices, health and nutrition guidelines, the process leading up to marriage, the specifics of discipline, and how to manage a home. An understanding of the difference between the Black and Whites and Grey areas is often crucial to unity within the body of Christ, for legalism frequently results in division. Not only can legalism be damaging to our relationships with one another, but it can also harm our witness to the lost when it becomes divisive. In John 13:35, Jesus said, "By this all people will know that you are my disciples, if you have love for one another."

Every word of God proves true;
he is a shield to those who take refuge in him.
Do not add to his words,
lest he rebuke you and you be found a liar.
–Proverbs 30:5, 6

It is important to realize that applications of commands are not commands themselves. For example, having your children use titles of respect (like Mr. and Mrs.) is an application of the Biblical instruction to respect one's elders (1 Timothy 5:1, 2). A number of adults in our social sphere have asked that our children call them by their first name or, when asked, have told us they didn't care either way. In such situations, having your child refer to an older person by their first name is simply a different application of the command to respect one's elders. Another example is structured family devotions: while it is a wonderful application of bringing our children up "in the discipline and instruction of the Lord" (Ephesians 6:4), it is not commanded.

Similarly, examples in Scripture are not the same as commands. Some claim that family-integrated worship (keeping all or most ages together during the entire church service) is a Biblical requirement because we see examples of it in Scripture, but examples are not prescriptive unless backed by a command. Yes, God commands parents to teach their children of Him, but many of the specifics of how to do so are Grey areas in which His Spirit will lead them as they follow Him. Parents who are seeking to love God with all of their hearts, souls, and minds (Matthew 22:37) will also desire for their children to do so, and they will be led by Him in the specifics of raising their family in the faith. Both age-integration and age-segregation in the church can be godly. Moreover, *both will be godly* when based on the clear commands of Scripture, and executed in the power and by the individual leading of the Holy Spirit.

If God leads us to do (or not do) something that is a Grey area, it then becomes sinful for us to do otherwise. James 4:17 says, "Whoever knows the right thing to do and fails to do it, for him it is sin." However, we have to be careful to never hold up a standard for others that God has given to us personally. Believers can start promoting their personal ways as God's universal way because we often have godly reasons for why we do what we do. There may even be Scriptures that the Lord used to lead us in a particular Grey area. And when we begin to experience the blessings of obedience to His leading, it is natural to want others to experience the same. The danger comes when we go beyond sharing our testimony about a particular tradition, to then holding up our way as *the* Biblical way. This is a form of legalism.

The word "legalism" is widely used (and misused) and can

mean different things to people, so it is important to clarify exactly what I mean by legalism in this book. One form of legalism is where a person tries to follow Old Testament law in order to be saved. Another kind of legalism is the belief that one must maintain their salvation by following Old Testament law, or certain aspects of it. The kind of legalism I am referring to in this book can be described as believing certain extrabiblical rules are God's universal standards of righteousness, and that those who obey them are godlier than those who do not. Regarding this, in his book, *The Bible Exposition Commentary,* Warren Wiersbe writes:

> *Legalism* is one of the major problems among Christians today. We must keep in mind that *legalism* does not mean the setting of spiritual standards; it means worshiping these standards and thinking that we are spiritual because we obey them. It also means judging other believers on the basis of these standards . . . The Pharisees had high standards; yet they crucified Jesus.[3]

I would add that this kind of legalism often mingles with another form of legalism when people begin to think their salvation is contingent upon keeping a myriad of rules. Salvation is by grace (God's unmerited favor toward us in Christ) alone, through faith alone (Ephesians 2:8).

Did you know that the Bible refers to *all* Christians as saints?

Eva (~6) said, "I have three names: my nickname, my real name . . . but 'Saint' is my favorite."

---

[3] Wiersbe, Warren W. *The Bible Exposition Commentary (Vol. 1).* Wheaton: Victor Books, 1996. 172.

In Matthew 15:3, Jesus chastised the Pharisees for breaking " 'the commandment of God for the sake of [their] tradition.' " One of the tragic consequences of legalism can be that we end up breaking God's actual commandments in order to follow an elevated tradition of men. Jesus went on to say that while the Pharisees honored Him with their lips, their hearts were, in fact, far from Him. Their worship of Him was in vain; they were teaching commandments of men as if they were from God (Matthew 15:8, 9).

Jerry Bridges wrote:

> Legalism insists on conformity to manmade religious rules and requirements, which are often unspoken but are nevertheless very real . . . There are far too many instances within Christendom where our traditions and rules are, in practice, more important than God's commands.[4]

Head Coverings and Homosexuality

But how do we make sure we are correctly interpreting the more difficult passages of Scripture and not disregarding any of God's commands? For example, what do we do with Paul's instruction to the Corinthian church for the married women to keep their heads covered whenever they prayed or prophesied during times of corporate worship (1 Corinthians 11:4–6)? Is it wrong that today the majority of Christian wives do not wear a veil? Are we rightly handling the Word in this regard? When studying the Bible, knowing about the culture to which the authors were speaking can be very helpful. Regarding this passage, notes in the ESV Study Bible say that "a woman's head covering in first-century Roman society

---

[4] Bridges, Jerry. *Transforming Grace: Living Confidently in God's Unfailing Love*. Carol Stream: NavPress, 2008. 144.

was a sign of marriage. . . . A married woman who uncovered her head in public would have brought shame to her husband."[5] During that time in the church, a woman's head covering was symbolic of her husband's authority over her (1 Corinthians 11:10), and it would have been disrespectful for her not to wear one. In our culture, wearing a veil does not communicate what it did back then, therefore, we do not have to wear head coverings today. But God's instructions for wives to submit to and respect their husbands are timeless principles (Colossians 3:18, 19; Ephesians 5:33).

I have heard the argument that Christians are being inconsistent by holding to the stance that homosexuality is a sin while disregarding the instruction to wear head coverings. However, there is no inconsistency. While head coverings were an application of a Biblical principle, the Bible makes it clear that the practice of homosexuality itself is wrong: "Because of this [referring to idolatry], God gave them over to shameful lusts. Even their women exchanged natural relations for those that are contrary to nature; and the men likewise gave up natural relations with women and were consumed with passion for one another, men committing shameless acts with men and receiving in themselves the due penalty for their error" (Romans 1:26, 27). Elsewhere, the Bible lists it amongst other sins (1 Corinthians 6:9, 10; 1 Timothy 1:8–10). Clearly, homosexuality is a sin regardless of time and culture. If we love those who have embraced this lifestyle, we will tell them the truth. Sadly, *tragically*, some churches and teachers are promoting homosexuality within the confines of a committed relationship and saying it is acceptable to God. If you are of this persuasion, I implore you not to fall into the deception of calling "evil good and good evil" (Isaiah 5:20). We must be uncompromising when it comes to the things God has clearly outlined in His Word, while making sure we always share such truths with gentleness and respect.

---

[5] Taken from the ESV® Study Bible (The Holy Bible, English Standard Version®), copyright ©2008 by Crossway, a publishing ministry of Good News Publishers. Used by permission. All rights reserved.

Understanding Old Testament Law

You may be wondering, as I often did, But what about all of the commands in the Old Testament (the laws that are found in the first five books of the Bible)? Are Christians supposed to abstain from eating pork? Should we rid our closets of all "clothing woven of two kinds of material" (Leviticus 19:19 NIV)? Is it a sin to go to church on Sunday since Saturday is the Jewish Sabbath? Certainly, children who curse their parents are no longer supposed to be put to death (Leviticus 20:9), right? I have learned there is a difference between the timeless moral laws of the Old Testament, which are reaffirmed in the New Testament ("do not murder," "do not commit adultery," "do not steal," etc.), and what are commonly referred to as the civil and ceremonial laws, which applied to the Jewish nation.

The civil laws were given to govern the people of ancient Israel (like those containing penalties for certain behaviors), while the ceremonial laws included instructions regarding the sacrificial system, clean and unclean foods, dress, etc. These laws not only served to set Israel apart from the surrounding pagan nations, but also pointed to Jesus and were fulfilled in His death and resurrection. Regarding festivals and Sabbaths, Colossians 2:17 says they are "a shadow of the things to come, but the substance belongs to Christ." Jesus said that He came not to destroy, but to fulfill the law (Matthew 5:17), and Romans 10:4 tells us that "Christ is the end of the law for righteousness to everyone who believes." The civil and ceremonial laws are not upheld in the New Testament, so, though still profitable for us to read and understand (2 Timothy 3:16, 17), they are not commands for us today. As it says in Romans 7:6, believers are "released from the law, having died to that which held us captive, so that we serve in the new way of the Spirit and not in the old way of the written code." Christians are "ministers of a new covenant" (2 Corinthians 3:6), for "God has done what the law, weakened by the flesh, could not do. By sending his own Son in the likeness of sinful flesh and for sin, he condemned sin in the flesh, in order that the righteous requirement of the law might be fulfilled in us, who walk not according to the flesh but according to the Spirit" (Romans 8:3, 4).

In 1 Corinthians 7:19, Paul says, "For neither circumcision counts for anything nor uncircumcision, but keeping the commandments of God." Circumcision represents the Old Covenant, while the "commandments of God" that Paul is referring to are His timeless moral laws coupled with other instructions for godly living found in the New Testament—all of which fall under the two great commandments to love God and others. Galatians 5:6 says that in Jesus "neither circumcision nor uncircumcision counts for anything, but only faith working through love." It is important to note that following the commands of God is neither a prerequisite for salvation nor a condition for staying saved; rather, it is an outworking of it. We are not saved by good works — we are saved *for* them. (If you would like to learn more about how Old Testament law relates to the New Covenant, I encourage you to read the book of Galatians.)

Look Not Only to [Your] Own Interests, but also to the Interests of Others -Philippians 2:4

When walking in various areas of freedom, we need to be careful not to cause a brother or sister to stumble into something they personally regard as sinful (Romans 14:21). Jesus said, " 'You shall love the Lord your God with all your heart and with all your soul and with all your mind. This is the great and first commandment. And a second is like it: You shall love your neighbor as yourself. On these two commandments depend all the Law and the Prophets.' " (Matthew 22:37–40). All of the Black and Whites of Scripture fulfill these two commandments, and, of course, every Grey area must also be subject to this law of love. Romans 13:10 says, "Love does no wrong to a neighbor; therefore *love is the fulfilling of the law*" (emphasis mine), and Galatians 6:2 says that by bearing one another's burdens we "fulfill the law of Christ." In matters of conscience, we need to make sure that we are choosing love over our liberties. Love always trumps freedom! As 1 Corinthians 8:4, 7–12 says:

> As to the eating of food offered to idols, we know that "an idol has no real existence," and that "there is no God but one.". . . . However, not all possess this knowledge. But some, through former association with idols, eat food as really offered to an idol, and their conscience, being weak, is defiled. Food will not commend us to God. We are no worse off if we do not eat, and no better off if we do. But take care that this right of yours does not somehow become a stumbling block to the weak. For if anyone sees you who have knowledge eating in an idol's temple, will he not be encouraged, if his conscience is weak, to eat food offered to idols? And so by your knowledge this weak person is destroyed, the brother for whom Christ died. Thus, sinning against your brothers and wounding their conscience when it is weak, you sin against Christ.

Some situations are easy to discern. For example, if your sister strongly believes that any alcohol consumption is sinful, don't pour yourself a glass of wine when you have her over for dinner. (To be clear, while drinking alcohol is not prohibited in Scripture, *getting drunk is*: Ephesians 5:18 says, "Do not get drunk with wine, for that is debauchery, but be filled with the Spirit." It is also important to note that there are many believers who, often due to personal or family histories of alcoholism, choose not to drink at all. Such decisions need to be respected.) But when it is not an obvious "weaker brother" issue, I encourage you to ask the Lord to lead you by His Spirit—He will.

Because the main message of this book concerns legalism, I may appear to be saying it is the only problem facing the church, but this is not the case. There are many dangers facing the church.

A prevalent one is licentiousness (a disregard for the commands of God), which is just as much a danger to the body of Christ as legalism is. We are prone to swing between these two dangerous extremes of legalism and license. The only way we can keep ourselves balanced in the middle, like Jesus, is to know the Word of God and obey it, in His power and for His glory. This is liberty—the place of "simplicity and purity *of devotion* to Christ" (2 Corinthians 11:3 NASB).

Licentiousness hurts families just as legalism does:

Sisters, we must remember that our enemy is "like a roaring lion, seeking someone to devour" (1 Peter 5:8).

His goal is to "steal and kill and destroy" (John 10:10): he wants to steal our good works by distracting us with fleshly desires, kill our witness for God by telling us it is okay to abuse grace, and destroy the relationships within our families by blinding us to the fact that sin hurts those around us.

As I write these things, I am so convicted! How often I forget that we do not live unto ourselves.

CHAPTER 2
Gently Led to Gently Lead

**My pastor, Nick Triveri, said,
"All Scripture is God-breathed—even the stuff left out."**

The fact that there are Grey areas raises the question, If God is
silent on some issues, then is the Word no longer sufficient for
all of life's decisions? But the sufficiency of Scripture is in no way
compromised by Grey areas, because the Word does "speak to all
of life" by giving us direction on how to proceed when the Bible is
not specific:

> Trust in the LORD with all your heart,
> And lean not on your own understanding;
> In all your ways acknowledge Him,
> and He shall direct your paths.
> –Proverbs 3:5, 6 NKJV

> "Ask, and it will be given to you;
> seek, and you will find;
> knock, and it will be opened to you.
> For everyone who asks receives,
> and the one who seeks finds,
> and to the one who knocks it will be opened."
> –Matthew 7:7, 8

> If any of you lacks wisdom, let him ask God,
> who gives generously to all without reproach,
> and it will be given him.
>
> –James 1:5

I believe one of the reasons the Bible is silent concerning some specifics in life is because God wants us *seeking Him* for direction. Let us not forget that Christianity is a relationship with the living God! Not only has He spoken to us clearly through His Word, but He has also given us His Spirit to live within us. These two Guides in our lives work together to lead us in "paths of righteousness for his name's sake" (Psalm 23:3).

When my friend Terry was a new convert and realized the Holy Spirit was living inside of her, she said to herself in amazement, "God has given me God!"

It is important to note that those of us who are called to be wives are to submit to our husbands (within Biblical parameters, of course—we should *never* submit to doing something sinful or that we have a personal conviction from the Lord about). When they lead in a particular Grey area that we may not agree with, we should share our concerns with them (and pray!), but as long as it is not something we feel our consciences stirred over, we are called to follow them. Easier said than done, *I know*, but God will give us the grace to submit, and He will bless this obedience.

Eva (~ 5) said, "Mom you are a-lot-of-charge, but Daddy is the most!"

For those of you raising your children without a husband, you may be a single parent, but you do not walk this path alone. God says He is the "father of the fatherless and protector of widows"

(Psalm 68:5). My sister Lisa became a widow before the birth of her son, and the Lord was faithful to lead her as she parented him by herself until she remarried more than four years later. Single moms, your job is big, but I pray you will remember that your God is bigger, and that He has a special heart for you and your little ones. Your Shepherd will carry you (Psalm 28:9).

Gently Led

Amidst the various struggles that parenting has presented me, one of the things I have struggled with the most has been wondering how the Lord wanted me to parent. For *so long*, I was "tossed to and fro" (Ephesians 4:14) by the multitude of teachings, suggestions, and opinions about mothering that seemed to be everywhere I turned! In Isaiah 54:11, God described the nation of Israel as an " 'afflicted one, storm-tossed and not comforted.' " This is an apt description of me during my stay in the prison of legalism. I frequently found myself blaming God for my confusion, and asking Him why He had burdened me with standards I could not reach. But nothing could have been further from the truth! "God is not a God of confusion" (1 Corinthians 14:33), and in Matthew 11:28-30, Jesus says, " 'Come to me, all who labor and are heavy laden, and I will give you rest. Take my yoke upon you, and learn from me, for I am gentle and lowly in heart, and you will find rest for your souls. For my yoke is easy, and my burden is light.' "

I used to be confused by these words "easy" and "light," because much of life is hard. Some lives are certainly harder than others, but no one alive will escape sin's realities. Dealing with the effects of the fall on creation, the world, the sin of others, and our own flesh is definitely no walk in the park. So, how can any of this be easy and light? I now know Jesus wasn't referring to life's hardships here; rather, I believe He was telling us that following Him is doable *in His strength*. First John 5:3 says, "For this is the love of God, that we keep his commandments. *And his commandments are not burdensome"* (emphasis mine). Compared to the heavy weight of legalism, following Jesus, empowered by the Spirit, is an easy yoke.

A note in the ESV Study Bible says this regarding a yoke:

> The wooden frame joining two animals . . . for pulling heavy loads was a metaphor for one person's subjection to another, and a common metaphor in Judaism for the law. The Pharisaic interpretation of the law, with its extensive list of proscriptions, had become a crushing burden . . . but was believed by the people to be of divine origin. Jesus' yoke of discipleship, on the other hand, brings **rest** through simple commitment to him . . . ."[6]

Faith like a child:

One day, feeling totally overwhelmed by my calling to parent seven children, I asked Zeke (7) *how* we were going to do it. Confidently, and without skipping a beat, he replied, "Easy-peasy!"

Strengthened by God's power, we can do all that He requires of us in His Word and leads us in by His Spirit. If we find ourselves burdened down with an "extensive list of proscriptions," we are no longer carrying Jesus' burden, but the oppressive and joyless yoke of legalism. This harsh spiritual existence is where I was for *so long*, but, by God's grace, I have come to know Him as a gentle Shepherd.

---

[6] Taken from the ESV® Study Bible (The Holy Bible, English Standard Version®), copyright ©2008 by Crossway, a publishing ministry of Good News Publishers. Used by permission. All rights reserved.

Charles Spurgeon said:

> Christ's reign in His church is that of a shepherd-king. He has supremacy, but it is the superiority of a wise and tender shepherd over His needy and loving flock; He commands and receives obedience, but it is the willing obedience of the well-cared-for sheep, rendered joyfully to their beloved Shepherd, whose voice they know so well. He rules by the force of love and the energy of goodness.[7]

My official "mommy verse" is Isaiah 40:11 (NIV):

> He tends his flock like a shepherd:
> He gathers the lambs in his arms
> and carries them close to his heart;
> he gently leads those that have young.

What a wonderful truth God has written on my heart through this verse! He will lead us gently—not in confusion or with impossible expectations. And following Jesus has a wonderful trickle-down effect: His gentle leading of us will translate into the gentle leading of our children, *if* we submit to His leadership. Apart from Christ, I have never been known as a gentle person. When I was a child, my dad referred to me as "a bull in a china shop," and it was a fitting description. This rough nature carried over into my mothering (There is a reason my kids hate getting their noses wiped!), and was only intensified by the extra-biblical rules I burdened myself with. Oh, how it grieves me that I have often led my children harshly and required of them more than they were capable of. God tells fathers not to provoke their children to anger (Ephesians 6:4), and Colossians 3:21 says, "Fathers, do not

---

[7] Spurgeon, Charles H. *Morning and Evening*. Peabody: Hendrickson Publishers, 1991. 464.

provoke your children, lest they become discouraged." Of course, this applies to mothers, as well. How much different would it have been for me and my kids if from the very beginning I had made gentleness a priority in my mothering, instead of the lesser things I mistakenly elevated for so long? Without love, getting places on time, going to church with brushed hair, and having clean floors means *nothing* (1 Corinthians 13:2).

While I now know that I know that *I know* love is the priority (meaning some things may not get done the way I like when I am putting people first), I still often struggle with keeping everything in its rightful place. I am so very thankful for God's grace that covers our sin and His working in our lives to make us more like Him! It is so important to remember that while we raise our kids, *God is raising us*. Let us learn from our mistakes—not focus on them. In Philippians 3:13 and 14, Paul wrote, "One thing I do: forgetting what lies behind and straining forward to what lies ahead, I press on toward the goal for the prize of the upward call of God in Christ Jesus."

Fear of Man + Legalism = *Disastrous* Parenting

Proverbs 29:25 warns us that "fear of man lays a snare." This sin has dominated most of my life. Basically, my flesh cares very much what you think about me, and I can attest to the fact that an outward, man-pleasing focus is fertile ground for legalism. In Matthew 23:25, Jesus accused the Pharisees of washing the outside of the cup while ignoring the weightier issues of the heart. One of the reasons they were guilty of this is because they sought to appear righteous for the praise of men. Jesus said that everything they did was done to be seen by others (Matthew 23:5). There were times I adopted legalistic standards because I cared desperately what others thought of me and my family. I may have been convinced that these things were required by God, as well, but my focus was not on pleasing Him.

> Am I now seeking the approval of man, or of God?
> Or am I trying to please man?
> If I were still trying to please man,
> I would not be a servant of Christ.
> –Galatians 1:10

Just like man-pleasing, legalism is predominantly concerned with outward performance. My fear of man, coupled with my legalistic tendencies, often caused me to focus solely upon the outside behavior of my children while ignoring the state of their hearts, which is always where true godliness originates. Jesus told the Pharisees to first " 'clean the inside of the cup . . . that the outside also may be clean' " (Matthew 23:26). Of course, I know I cannot change the hearts of my children and that I must train them according to what is right, but, as I do so, I must always look to God to do the work in their hearts that *only He can do*. He alone can save them. And He alone can change them from the inside out that they might bear genuine fruit—not fake fruit that only exists to make us look good.

An excellent article about the dangers of parenting with a focus on the outside is "Solving the Crisis in Homeschooling"[8] by Reb Bradley. It was written for homeschoolers, but the principles apply to all parents.

When I am living for what people think about me, and adopting oppressive legalistic standards in the process, it has disastrous ramifications in how I portray the Christian life to my children. Not only can it push a child away from God and toward a life of prodigal living, it can also lead them from Him in the more subtle way of encouraging them to be little Pharisees. Pharisees may often be

---

[8] Bradley, Reb. "Solving the Crisis in Homeschooling," accessed February 13, 2018, http://www.familyministries.com/HS Crisis.htm.

easier to raise than prodigals because their sin is less apparent, but they are both on dangerous and ungodly paths. Turning from the sin of man-pleasing and throwing off the binding shackles of legalism frees us to emphasize in our parenting the things that truly matter! May we all, by God's grace, be parents who parent unto Him alone, who seek to hear "well done" from Him alone, and who model before our children a fear of God alone.

Follow the Leader

Something I often refer to throughout this book is the Lord's leading of His children. This is something that is clearly spoken about in the Bible. In Romans 8:14, we are told that "all who are led by the Spirit of God are sons of God," and Galatians 5:18 says, "If you are led by the Spirit, you are not under the law." (According to a note in the ESV Study Bible, the word used for "led" here is a verb that "implies an active, personal involvement by the Holy Spirit in guiding Christians, and the present tense . . . indicates . . . ongoing activity."[9]) The Bible also gives us specific examples of the Spirit leading: Jesus was led by the Spirit into the wilderness (Matthew 4:1). In Acts 8:29, we are told "the Spirit said to Philip, 'Go over and join this chariot.' " The Lord also led Paul, Silas, and Timothy by His Spirit: "And they went through the region of Phrygia and Galatia, having been forbidden by the Holy Spirit to speak the word in Asia. And when they had come up to Mysia, they attempted to go into Bithynia, but the Spirit of Jesus did not allow them. So, passing by Mysia, they went down to Troas. And a vision appeared to Paul in the night: a man of Macedonia was standing there, urging him and saying, 'Come over to Macedonia and help us.' And when Paul had seen the vision, immediately we sought to go on into Macedonia, concluding that God had called us to preach the gospel to them"

---

[9] Taken from the ESV® Study Bible (The Holy Bible, English Standard Version®), copyright © 2008 by Crossway, a publishing ministry of Good News Publishers. Used by permission. All rights reserved.

(Acts 16:6–10). And in Acts 20:22, Paul said he was compelled by the Spirit to go to Jerusalem. Our Shepherd leads!

I wrote the following poem early-on in my parenting journey, and the Lord has often used it to encourage me—not only in the face of my many failures as a mom, but to remind me to follow His gentle leading so that I might gently lead my children to Him. May it serve as an encouragement for you too (At the end of this chapter, there is a bookmark to cut out with this poem on it.):

Little Lambs

I'll never be a perfect mom,
But You, O Lord, are perfect in me.
Above all of my faults and flaws,
May it be You in me they see.
Hold my hand while I hold theirs,
So I can take them where You lead.
Lord, You've blessed me with Your little lambs;
As I shepherd them,
Shepherd me.

All of the illustrations in this book, which were drawn by my daughters Esther (~13) and Eva (~11), are of shepherds and sheep. That theme came about from this poem and Isaiah 40:11, and it is such a powerful metaphor for our relationship with the Lord. We are all just simple, little sheep in desperate need of our Shepherd to lead us: John 10:3 tells us that He "calls his own sheep by name and leads them out."

Leading Looks Like . . .?

God leads His children through the Grey areas of life in a myriad of ways! One way I am frequently led is by simply having peace (or a lack of peace) when making decisions and walking in areas of freedom.

Some other ways I have been directed by the Lord are: through passages of Scripture that I just know apply to a certain situation, by "hearing" Him speak (either through Spirit-inspired thoughts or what I would describe as a strong impression in my spirit), through circumstances meant to guide me in a particular direction, by open and closed doors, and through the counsel of others (often my husband). There are times He leads me through various combinations of these, and I also believe I am often led without even being aware.

> I will instruct you and teach you in the way you should go;
> I will counsel you with my eye upon you.
> –Psalm 32:8

I don't want to give the impression that following God's leading is something I have mastered. *Far from it.* Not only have I often failed to follow due to sin, but I am still growing in my ability to recognize His leading. There are times I struggle discerning whether I am hearing His voice or my own thoughts and feelings, I can still get confused by legalism (which seriously clouds my understanding of His will for my life), and it isn't always clear to me if I am interpreting things, like open doors, correctly. But I can rest in His grace and goodness to guide me *despite myself.* If we truly want to know and do His will, will He not lead us to it one way or another? I also believe that the more we follow Him, the more we will grow in being able to more readily discern His leading in our lives.

I want to make it clear that by sharing examples from my walk with the Lord, I am not defining what His leading looks like in everyone's life. While I can encourage you to be led by the Lord, I cannot give you a set of steps to follow, because following after the Shepherd is not a program—*it is a relationship.* And just as our relationships with our individual children are unique, God relates to each of us in personal ways.

Something I *can* tell you to do is to be quick to acknowledge and turn from sin. This is a key element to following the Lord's leading. Before Jesus said that His yoke is easy and His burden is light, He told us to learn from Him for He is " 'gentle and lowly in heart' " (Matthew 11:29). Other versions translate the word "lowly" as humble. Jesus never had any sin to confess, but humility for us often requires admission of sin. First John 1:8 and 9 says, "If we say we have no sin, we deceive ourselves, and the truth is not in us. If we confess our sins, he is faithful and just to forgive us our sins and to cleanse us from all unrighteousness." (This confession of sin in the life of a believer keeps us in close communion with God; sin disrupts our fellowship with Him.) We cannot run this race well if we are not consistently putting off what Hebrews 12:1 in the NIV refers to as the "sin that so easily entangles." (I have had to learn this *the hard way* . . .) Not only that, but Hebrews 3:13 warns us not to be "hardened by the deceitfulness of sin." This hardness refers to a heart of unbelief (v.12), which would cause us to stop running the race altogether. May we never fail to see the destructive and dangerous nature of our sin, and may God give us the grace to hate it as He does.

I can also encourage you to ask the Lord to lead you. After having asked God to search him, David ended Psalm 139 with the petition—"lead me in the way everlasting!" Another important part of following Jesus is *seeking to be led* by Him. Hebrews 11:6 tells us that God rewards those who seek Him. Jesus taught us to ask God in prayer for His will to be done, on earth as it is in heaven (Matthew 6:10). If we are not in that place of seeking His leading, we can easily be deceived by our flesh, the world, or the enemy of our souls. As it says in 1 John 4:1, "Beloved, do not believe every spirit, but test the spirits to see whether they are from God, for many false prophets have gone out into the world." We can do so through prayer and the full counsel of God's Word. Romans 12:2 says, "Do not be conformed to this world, but be transformed by the renewal of your mind, that by testing you may discern what is the will of God, what is good and acceptable and perfect." A good question to ask in order to guard ourselves against deception from ourselves is, Are we seeking " 'first the kingdom of God and his righteousness' " (Matthew 6:33)? Another one is, Am I trying to "discern what is pleasing to the Lord" (Ephesians 5:10)?

Laura Ellis

It is my hope and prayer that you will come to, or continue to, know the Lord as the Good Shepherd in your day-to-day life. May we all experience the blessed peace that comes from surrendering to His gentle leading!

> Teach me to do your will, for you are my God!
> Let your good Spirit lead me on level ground!
> –Psalm 143:10

Where I am disciplined by the Lord and led through closed doors:

Over-commitment is something I became particularly prone to after my youngest child was potty-trained and I entered into a new season of life. With teenagers in the house that could now babysit, I was able to run to the store *by myself* (gasp) in the middle of the day. With all of this newfound freedom, I also found myself available to serve in a multitude of ways I hadn't been able to before. A number of these things I know the Lord had called me to, but there were also some I committed to apart from His leading. One particularly packed week, I had three people cancel on me for separate engagements and my week was still super busy. (It seems I had forgotten I still parent seven children and have a husband who is really fond of dinner . . .) Those three closed doors were a wake-up call that I needed to slow down and be more prayerful about the things I so readily say yes to. "Slow to speak and quick to pray" is my new motto.

You can cut this out to use as a bookmark:

Little Lambs
By, Laura Ellis

I'll never be a
perfect mom,
But You, O Lord,
are perfect in me.
Above all of my
faults and flaws,
May it be You in
me they see.
Hold my hand while
I hold theirs,
So I can take them
where You lead.
Lord, You've blessed me
with Your little lambs;
As I shepherd them,
Shepherd me.

CHAPTER 3
Love Is the Goal

**Elijah's (4) version of "I love you to death" was
"I love you *so that you will be so dead!*"**

The legalistic teachings about order that I struggled with regarding my babies, carried over into how I viewed managing my home. Even as I came to realize that infant scheduling isn't a Biblical command, I had subconsciously internalized in my mind that following a daily schedule was the most godly way to run a family. The problem was that I am not oriented that way (although I so admire those of you that are). We followed this basic routine for a long time: get up and eat breakfast, do some things we need to do, eat lunch, do more things that need to get done, get through that insane hour or so before dinner when everyone seems to be either whinier or wilder (*or both*), eat dinner, clean up, have family time, get the kids to bed, probably have some time together, and then go to sleep. And several years ago, we added some more structure to our routine, but scheduling things to the half hour? To me, it has always felt like swimming up river . . . in the middle of the night . . . during a thunderstorm . . . with my hands tied behind my back. It just doesn't work. (But I know it *will* work if the Lord ever leads me to do so—because He will be in it.)

Angus Buchan, the South African farmer-turned-preacher whose life inspired the must-see movie *Faith Like Potatoes,*[10] said, "We need to do what He's told us to do—no more, no less."[11]

No more. No less.

Off and on, usually depending upon what I had read or whom I had talked to that week, I would feel as if I was failing God, because I just could not run my household in a more controlled manner. I couldn't seem to shake the nagging thoughts that He was disappointed with me, and that I was a lousy wife, a lazy mom, and a lesser Christian than those that adhered to schedules. In fact, there were so many times I got to the place where I felt absolutely hopeless, as if none of my efforts as a mother meant anything if I couldn't get a schedule down. (This is faulty logic, of course, but it shows how much legalism in this area dominated my thinking and affected my daily life.) How wonderful to finally realize that daily scheduling is a Grey area. Sure, schedules and routines can be helpful tools (and to some are absolutely indispensable), but they are not *the way* to manage your home.

I have heard the argument made that we are to strive for order with time because "God is a God of order." Yes, absolutely, He is a God of order, but the only order I see Him commanding us to in the New Testament is in regard to submission to authorities, our family relationships, and the structure of church government and worship. How we go about our day-to-day activities is a Grey area that He will be faithful to lead us in as we follow Him.

---

[10] Rautenbach, Frank, Hamilton Dhlamini, and Jeanne Wilhelm. *Faith Like Potatoes.* DVD. Directed by Regardt Van Den Bergh. South Africa: Global Creative Studios, 2008.
[11] Buchan, Angus, Anton Dekker, Lucky Koza, Jaco Muller, Anrich Herbst, Robin Smith, Hannes Muller, David James, Kate Normington, and Michelle Douglas. *Angus Buchan's Ordinary People.* DVD. Directed by FC Hamman and C.A. Van Aswegen. South Africa: FC Hamman Films, 2012.

You may be wondering, But aren't we commanded to redeem the time? Yes, the Bible tells us to "walk, not as unwise but as wise, making the best use of the time, because the days are evil" (Ephesians 5:15, 16). Wisdom has often been defined as "knowledge applied," and the Bible tells us that the fear of the Lord is the beginning of wisdom (Proverbs 9:10 NIV). "The fear of the Lord" refers to having reverence for Him. I would define "walking wisely" as the result of being in a right relationship with God, knowing Him and His Word, and applying that knowledge to our lives under the guidance of the Spirit. Doing what God leads us to do is how we make the best use of our time! Jesus was always about His Father's business; this is to be the aim of our days too. And if you are led to do so by following a schedule, what a blessing it will be to you! Just know, it is not a universal command.

> Who is the man who fears the Lord?
> Him will he instruct in the way that he should choose.
> –Psalm 25:12

I no longer wring my hands over our lack of a schedule, because I know God will be faithful to lead us in the level of order that is right (and light) for our individual family. Our God hung the stars in place and told the ocean waves where to stop, so He can certainly show us how to run our family in each season of life! It may not always look pretty, and fingernails (including mine) may get overlooked from time to time, but the Lord looks at the heart (1 Samuel 16:7), right?

When I accidentally scratched Elijah (4) with my fingernail, he said, "Ow! You got me with your sharp claw!"

29

Order with things is a Grey area too. Stuff organization can be helpful, but it is not commanded anywhere in the Bible. The saying "a place for everything, and everything in its place" is *not* Scripture, but for someone like me who excels at organizing things, it can feel akin to something sacred. I can easily fall into legalism in this area because I absolutely love the idea of keeping various items sorted in little, labeled boxes all lined up neatly on a shelf. *For joy!* (I once read that Christians should pick up and put away any item they pass by that is out of place. I'm assuming the person who wrote that probably has the same natural bent that I do, so to him it seemed right, but that is a man's standard—not God's.) There have been times I have looked at my sister Lisa, who does not delight in sorting like I do, and thought something along the lines of, *Just do it!* But just like I can't "just follow" a schedule, she can't "just keep" her Sippy cup shelf in order because it is not her natural bent. The Lord is leading her in the level of order that is right for her. Of course, He could change her into someone who delights in alphabetizing her spices . . . *or not.* He is the Shepherd; He will lead. All she needs to do is follow.

There is an old poem by an anonymous author entitled "Do the Next Thing." Elisabeth Elliot often used the phrase "do the next thing" in her speaking and writing. I *love* this! However, there was a time when the idea of simply doing what was next was troubling to me, because us mamas often have a number of seemingly "next things" to do. If the baby is crying, the soup is burning, your kids are fighting, the phone is ringing, and the toddler needs a diaper change, you might very well wonder what to do next! But I have come to find much peace in knowing the Lord will lead as we walk in step with the Spirit.

If you are led to schedule your day to the half hour, great! If following more of a sequential flow to your day (a routine) is God's plan for you, great! And if He has shown you the best way for you to manage your time is by just getting up and doing the things the Spirit directs you to do as you go along, great! Is color-coding Legos your thing? Go for it! For those of you that just got a headache reading about sorting 3,672,541 Legos by color, go ahead and shove them all together into a giant tub (or plastic kiddie pool). Or just turn your kid's room into a "Lego Room," meaning they never get picked up. There are a myriad of ways to run a home, and it is my prayer that each one of us will find the unique way to manage ours that God has called us to and equipped us for.

My friend Page often prays that she would be "alert, attentive, and available." I love this, and remind my girls of these three words when they go to babysit somewhere. This is how we are to be as servants of the Lord: alert to His voice, attentive to His leading, and available to do *whatever* He calls us to.

I Think I Can, I Think I Can . . . *I Think I Can?*

Mickey was trying to help Elijah (4) go down the fireman's pole at the park. Elijah said, "I want to . . . but my body is scared."

But does acknowledging that we have weaknesses in certain areas negate the truth that we "can do all things through him who strengthens [us]" (Philippians 4:13)? Could weaknesses in areas like organization and time management really just be signs of laziness or a lack of faith? First, we need to understand that this verse is referring to all the things *we are called to do.* Secondly, only God truly understands the complexities of our human makeup. He will convict us of our sin, and He is in the business of growing all of His children, but we cannot lose sight of the fact that many of our weaknesses may be by design—*not* speaking about sin here, of course. (And some things that we regard as weaknesses may not even be considered as such in God's economy!) If we are weak in some area for a purpose, we can trust the Lord to use it for good in our lives. Paul said he boasted about his weaknesses because God's strength was made perfect in them (2 Corinthians 12:7–10).

We need to remember that His thoughts are not our thoughts, and His ways are not our ways (Isaiah 55:8):

- He enabled Sarah to become pregnant and give birth to a son in her and Abraham's old age (Genesis 21:2).
- He weakened Jacob's hip (Genesis 32:24–32).
- He chose Israel to be His people even though they were "the fewest of all the peoples" (Deuteronomy 7:7, 8).
- He used a man "slow of speech and of tongue" to lead His people out of bondage in Egypt (Exodus 4:10–16).
- He used a small stone in a shepherd's sling to kill a giant (1 Samuel 17).
- He reduced Gideon's army . . . *twice* (Judges 7:1–8).
- He chose Bethlehem, which was "too little to be among the clans of Judah" (Micah 5:2), as the place where the Son of God would be born.
- He took a rough fisherman and raised him up to be a leader in His church (Matthew 4:18–20).
- He used a man who was "unskilled in speaking" to bring the Gospel to the Gentiles (2 Corinthians 11:6).
- He distributed a variety of gifts to His body for the building up of everybody, and said that "the parts of the body that seem to be weaker are indispensable" (1 Corinthian 12:22).

Not many wise, mighty, or noble are called, you know—"God chose what is foolish in the world to shame the wise; God chose what is weak in the world to shame the strong; God chose what is low and despised in the world, even things that are not, to bring to nothing things that are, so that no human being might boast in the presence of God" (1 Corinthians 1:26–29).

So, let's stop focusing on our weaknesses, and allow Him to make us into the vessels *He* wants us to be for the unique purposes He has for each one of us. Surrender to God's will, not striving for our own definitions of perfection, is the key to growth in this Christian life. Sisters, we can trust in His power to change us into the image of Christ from "one degree of glory to another" (2 Corinthians 3:18), to equip us for our individual functions within the church, and to lead us in paths of righteousness for the glory of His name.

Control Is *Not* the Goal

Esther wrote this in our book of family quotes:

"Our house rule is Love is the goal. [And] always to remember Jesus Saves."

Not only did I struggle with schedules, but keeping order in other areas was a burden that weighed heavily upon me for some time, as well. Mickey was praying for me one day, and God spoke something to his spirit concerning my struggle with feeling that I needed to be in absolute control of everything (time, stuff, children) in order to truly be pleasing to Him. What was impressed upon his heart was: Control is not the goal—*love is*. I now frequently ask my children "What is the goal?" and have since put wooden plaques and chalkboards that say "LOVE" in various places of my home so that, wherever I happen to be looking from, I can have a visual reminder that love is the goal—not control. I truly believe it was a prophetic word for me. (Of course, parents are to have a certain level of control over their children. This is not what I'm referring to.) While our spirits long for a perfect world (which is coming, by the way!), the reality is, we live in a messy, broken place with messy, broken people. Trying to control it all only drives us crazy and drives others away, but when we are walking in love, and letting the Lord lead in all the particulars, we will *always* succeed. (Even if, from the outside, it looks like everything is falling apart.)

My mom collects "heart rocks" (rocks she finds in the shape of a heart) and puts them in glass bowls around her house. She even took some of her best ones, glued them to a piece of cardboard, and framed it. I would love to do this one day as another visual reminder to love.

Love at the Table

Another area I was tossed over was manners. There is quite a bit of legalistic teaching out there that holds up certain forms of etiquette as if they are standards of righteousness. For years, I felt like a failure as a parent because my children lacked certain social graces that I thought were essential in a Christian family. (Although, it really should not have come as a surprise since I confess I am still working on my own table manners . . . *I'm just a really late bloomer, okay?* Seriously though, I have found myself super frustrated with my children over things, only to realize later that I struggle in the same areas. Parenting can be very humbling!) While manners can be very good ways to apply God's command to love, it is important to remember that they are not moral laws. Manners are social rules that can vary from time period to time period, culture to culture, family to family, person to person, and even situation to situation.

How I rued the day "stupid" found its way into my kid's vocabulary. Up until that point, the name of choice had been "Googly Eye." As in, "You took my Lego, *Googly Eye!*" (I know name-calling like this is unkind, but, I have to admit, it made me laugh from time to time.)

In 1 Corinthians 13:5, where love is defined as not being rude, the idea is not that love strictly adheres to social formalities, but that love "does not behave in an ugly, indecent, unseemly, or unbecoming manner."[12] The Greek word translated "rude" is used only one other time in the New Testament (1 Corinthians 7:36), where it refers to a man who "thinks that he is not behaving properly toward his betrothed."[13] I believe both Scriptures are referring to clear inappropriate behavior—conforming to every societal tradition could not have been the point. Jesus and His disciples did not follow all the traditions of their day (Matthew 9:14; 15:1, 2; Luke 11:38), and they sometimes offended the Pharisees in the process. We use the word "rude" liberally in our culture. Much behavior that is considered rude is not sinful in and of itself. For example, slurping while eating cereal is not a sin, but when my younger son does it on purpose to irritate his older brother, he is definitely not walking in love. When we are walking in love, we *will* fulfill the law. We have to trust the Spirit to show us what is truly rude, and let Him lead us as we navigate the waters of whatever culture and individual situation we find ourselves in. As it says in Psalm 5:8, we can pray, "Lead me, O Lord, in your righteousness . . . make your way straight before me."

There is much peace in trusting God's leading in my life, as opposed to the various legalistic teachings that permeated my thinking. I still struggle at times, but overall, I can say that it has been wonderful to be set free! My passion is that others might avoid the painful process I went through as I was tossed about by legalism. With God's Word as our plumb line, we can avoid being "carried about by every wind of doctrine, by human cunning, by craftiness in deceitful schemes" (Ephesians 4:14).

Parenting according to God's commands is a big enough task without adding instructions He has not given. And His Biblical commands to parents are clear:

---

[12] Spiros, Zodhites Th.D. *The Complete Word Study Dictionary: New Testament.* Chattanooga: AMG Publishers, 1992. 284.
[13] Ibid.

- Children are to obey and honor their parents (Ephesians 6:1-3).
- Fathers are to be careful not to provoke their children and to "bring them up in the discipline and instruction of the Lord" (Ephesians 6:4).
- Mothers are to love their children with a *phileo* (affectionate) love (Titus 2:4).

Then, there are all the other areas in which God will lead us individually. Do not forget that Jesus said His burden is light. If you find yourself burdened by standards that God has not given in His Word, I encourage you to pray about them. Make sure they are part of His gentle leading on your parenting journey.

Eva memorized Ephesians 6:1 in her sweet toddler way: "Obey–parents–Lord– right."

Methods *Must* Be Subject to the Master

Even if God leads you to a particular parenting method, I encourage you to hold onto it loosely. Please know, I am not trying to dissuade anyone from following methods—my heart is to simply share the importance of making sure they are always subject to His leadership. I learned this one evening a number of years ago: One of my daughters was throwing a tantrum. We felt the Lord had led us in a certain method for dealing with such behavior, but that night I felt it impressed upon my heart to just hold her and pray. I hesitated at first (because . . . *The Method!*), but the Lord made it clear to me that the best way to love her right then was not with discipline. Not only was that exactly what was needed for the moment, but it was also a very powerful lesson for me that I need to trust the Master and not the method. He will always lead us to keep love as the goal.

Love will find a way:

My kids were watching a movie while I rested on the couch, and Ezra (3) kept kissing me on the cheek. I asked him to stop so I could rest a little. He was not to be deterred: I opened my eyes to find him blowing me kisses!

However you are led to manage your time, maintain your stuff, and mother your children, please remember, control is not the goal—love is. It is *always* the most excellent way.

We love because *He first loved us* (1 John 4:19):

After having written this chapter, I realized something was missing—the starting point! We can only love because He loved us first: "God shows his love for us in that while we were still sinners, Christ died for us" (Romans 5:8). He has loved us "with an everlasting love" (Jeremiah 31:3), and it is because of His love that we are "called children of God" (1 John 3:1). I should also mention that the Bible tells us God *is* love. It was said of Jesus at Lazarus' tomb: "Behold how he loved him!" (John 11:36 KJV) Knowing we are *so loved*, encourages us to love well with the same love that we have been shown. "Love is the goal" will be nothing more than a mere sentiment unless we allow Jesus to pour out His love for others through us.

CHAPTER 4
Different by Design

Eva (6) kept writing notes to people—one morning, she
made three for Mickey alone! I had to ask her to stop
because I was running out of notecards.
"But Mommy!" she protested.
"That's what Evas do!"

My battle with legalism began with a book and was perpetuated
by many more. "To [read] or not to [read]?" is a question I
should have been asking myself long ago, but I approached reading
the way Eva did cards—it was just something I did. Being an avid
thrift store shopper as a young wife and mother, I read *many*
Christian books written by women for women. I gleaned much
solid teaching and numerous helpful tips from a good number of
these books, however, sometimes the author's opinions were put
forth as *the way* to be a godly woman. This would often send me
into a whirlwind of confusion. (I'm sure it's obvious by now that I
am extremely sensitive to written material that carries legalistic
tones. What some may be able to sift through with discernment,
can become for others a minefield of confusion and doubt.)

Some of my little ones kept getting into Esther's (6) desk. She complained
to me, most passionately, that there wasn't *"one sparkly thing left!"* in there.

Even after I learned the difference between people's opinions and God's revealed will, I still struggled with the comparison trap. Nowhere was this harder than when I read about the lives of others. We, as twenty-first century women, have more information readily available (via the Internet) than any other previous generation. How easy it is to get caught up comparing our lives with the way others are doing home life, but 2 Corinthians 10:12 says, "When they measure themselves by one another and compare themselves with one another, *they are without understanding*" (emphasis mine). Failing to heed this truth, I got caught up wondering whose way was "best," but what is best for one family, may not be God's best for another. (And what is best for us in one season of life, might not be God's will in another season.)

Many well-meaning women may give you practical advice based on their personal convictions, unique situations, callings, strengths, and spiritual giftings. However, we need to remember that not only were we created differently and, as believers, given "gifts that differ according to the grace given to us" (Romans 12:6), but we are also often in very different places in life. Therefore, what works for one woman may not work for another. I struggled with one author's writings, in particular, until I finally realized she was writing from the perspective and experience of raising one child. Practically speaking, she was able to do things that I am simply not called to do with seven kids.

Eva (~3) liked using double negatives: "I not like it! *No!*"

Oh, BOY!

Parenting advice from a mother of all girls is probably going to be very different than that given by a mother with only boys. I like to jokingly say that people should not write parenting books unless they have raised a boy. But truthfully, my advice to other parents would be very different if I only had the experience of raising my girls (and vice versa), because they are *just different.*

---

*When Esther (2) would play with toy cars, instead of making car sounds like her brother, she would cradle hers and shush it saying, "He's crying. He's crying."

*I once found Eva (4) playing "Mommy and Kid" with a John Deere tractor and a Matchbox car.

My girls generally play in a more subdued manner than their brothers. When Elijah (8) was away for over a week, the house was noticeably quieter and calmer without him in it. Within about *an hour* of his returning home, he had turned an entire bedroom into a "jet" (using chairs, desks, and ropes), and the noise level had spiked drastically! This is the same child who asked me, at the age of five, "Do you want me to turn my energy on or off?" By God's grace, I have come to see that many of these differences in my boys are part of His design. (Yes, even some of those things that tend to drive me *more than a little crazy*— and, by His grace, I am learning to appreciate His purposes in them.)

Miniature Men:

*Zeke (~ 4) fell down and I asked him if it hurt. "No," he replied, grinning. "That didn't hurt—*because I am a man!*"

*Zeke (3) asked me to feel his arm muscle. I did and said, "Ooooh." He nodded his head knowingly and said, "I know."

Of course, not all boys are bursting with energy, and some girls can really keep us mamas on our toes. I have one daughter who *loves* to climb things . . . and she has the scars to prove it! If there is a column somewhere, she is the first one who will attempt to shimmy her way up it. She once warned her grandpa: "If you tickle me, I'll climb you!" One day, I even caught her climbing the outside wall of an automotive store: Mickey and I had each taken half of our kids that morning to run separate errands. I had no idea he was going there, and was sitting in a nearby drive-thru when Zeke saw her scaling the wall from across the parking lot. Imagine her surprise when she heard me yell from out of nowhere for her to *"get down!"*

The legendary antics of my son Zeke (in his early years):

- Took his newborn sister outside, laid her on the deck, and just left her there
- Partially soaked the living room carpet with a hose—twice!
- Sprayed me full-on with a hose—not once, not twice, but three times
- Broke his big brother's CD player, and then broke the new replacement the *very day* it was purchased
- Required us to buy more gates and door locks than we had for our first three children combined!
- Sharpied and Sharpied and Sharpied things *so not meant for Sharpies*—like leather ottomans. (I have a love/hate relationship with that pen . . .)
- On one shopping trip: squished bananas into the plastic holes of the cart; scattered a container of mushrooms all throughout the cart; opened two boxes of packaged oatmeal and proceeded to drop the individual packets down the floor of an aisle; and then grabbed and frantically tried to open some Mentos in the checkout line before I caught him. (And these are just the things I remembered to write down later!)

- Woke me up one morning by dousing me with a *cold* cup of water
- Another time, I woke up to him asking what was more dangerous: "poison or dynamite?"
- Got lost at church a number of times
- Got lost again by hiding under some flotation devices during a church baptism at our city pool, which not only disrupted things but *nearly killed me*
- Took a nap in a hidden place, causing me to panic and call 9-1-1 (the operator actually asked if they should send out an ambulance—*for me*)
- Called 9-1-1 and caused them to believe it was a hostage situation because he was whispering. They even showed up in SWAT gear!
- Super-glued his lips together
- Stuck a metal key in an outlet and got seriously shocked (as in, thrown to the ground)
- Took condiments out of the fridge and threw them over the backyard fence
- Ran around the house poking unsuspecting siblings with a sharpened pencil
- And ate some dog food (which, obviously, was the least of my worries!)

My kids were playing "David and Goliath" one day. I thought it was so cute, and was happy they were acting out a Bible story, until Elijah (~5), using a burp cloth as a sling, flung *an actual rock* across the room.

My friend Faith Alterton put together a "Very Good Baby Shower Gifts for Mothers of Boys List" on her blog. The following are some of the things she listed:

1. **Wall Spackle**—The best kind is . . . in a nice little squeeze tube. For easy, frequent repairs.
2. **Stud-finder**—Because if it goes on a wall, it needs to be in a stud with a 2" screw. Curtain rods, wall hooks, TP holders, pictures. Trust me, just find the studs.
3. **Goof-off**—'Nough said. Removes just about everything but permanent marker which is sadly, quite permanent.
4. **Wax Rings**—You know, for when you've been searching for the toothbrush for five minutes and your toddler wonders aloud whether it might be in the toilet still. And the sluggish flush suddenly makes a lot of sense. Always keep at least two of them. And maybe a snake.
5. **Compression Dressings**—For head lacerations, of which you'll have plenty. They bleed like crazy and are usually in places where Band-Aids won't go, like hair. I like to use a narrow ace wrap to hold a pad of gauze in place. It frees your hands for comforting, and cleanup.
6. ***National Audubon Society Field Guide to North American Insects and Spiders***[14]—It's just better to know their names. Trust me. As in, "Isaac, just where do you think you're going with that sweet little root borer?" Lends dignity to a discussion. (I'm really, really glad we don't live in Indonesia with guys like these. Really glad.)
7. **Sturdy Rubber Boots and a Superman cape**—And maybe a set for the boy.

All humor aside, please don't think that I am saying it is easier to raise girls! While it is true that boys tend to be more active with all of the resulting consequences, such things can pale in comparison to a meltdown over a bad pedicure: I buy the fast-drying nail polish and apply it with a multitude of warnings to be

---

[14] Lorus and Margery, Milne, and Susan Rayfi eld. *National Audubon Society Field Guide to North American Insects and Spiders.* New York: Alfred A. Knopf, a division of Random House Inc., 1980.

still, yet we always seem to have something like a smudged pinky toe that elicits cries of dismay. And frequent wrestling can be more bearable than a fight over "the dress" in the dress-up bin. (I have a very vivid memory of an epic battle I had with one of my sisters over *one* article of clothing that I was *convinced* held the key to my happiness at school the next day.) So, whether you have only boys, all girls, one of each, just one, or some of both, I know it is hard. Wonderful, beautiful, and yes, *hard!*

Not All Men like Lipstick

Godly older women are instructed to "train the young women to love their husbands and children, to be self-controlled, pure, working at home, kind, and submissive to their own husbands, that the word of God may not be reviled" (Titus 2:4, 5). My mom often teaches the women at our church that it is important to note the text says "to love," not "*how* to love." Please don't get me wrong, How To's can be great, and God wants us to have teachable hearts that can learn from others (Proverbs 27:17 says, "Iron sharpens iron, and one man sharpens another."), but there are a myriad of different ways to apply Titus 2 to our lives! One reason for this is explained in verse five: women are to be "submissive to *their own* husbands" (emphasis mine). I love how Scripture interprets Scripture! Each husband has his own desires for how he wants his home and family life to run; therefore, these verses cannot mean younger women are to be subject to older women's opinions regarding the particulars (the Grey areas) of life. Another sister can tell me to be gentle in the way I instruct my children because that is a clear Biblical teaching, but she shouldn't tell me I *have to* apply lipstick before I greet my husband at the end of the day. I have read in several places the importance of applying lipstick before your husband gets home from work, but Mickey prefers that I not wear it, so I should obey his wishes, as opposed to the opinions of others. (At least once, he came home to find me wearing it as I stood by the front door to greet him and instantly knew I had read a new book!)

A friend of mine wrote, "I went through a season where I decided [my husband] was going to be the "king" of our home and deferred to him on every single detailed decision. This came from a woman I knew and also a book I had read. One day [he] told me, "Just decide!" and I realized that this was not the way he wanted to live. He wants to come home from work and have things taken care of. He's happy that I decide things, not big stuff, of course, but he doesn't want to be asked about every little thing . . . It boiled down to me listening to and caring what others thought more than what the Lord was directing us in personally as a family. . . . I've learned, yes, I am submissive toward and defer to my husband, but it doesn't look like the one-size-fits-all dictate I was trying to squeeze us into, and that's ok!"

Another thing my husband (the social rebel) is opposed to is making beds. And what did I often read about in my early years of being a wife and mother? Making beds. I still read and hear about it. Since Mickey thinks bed making is unnecessary, he has requested that we not do it. I *finally* made peace with the fact that it really is God's best for us to have unmade beds, but it was a battle for some time: Was there some incredibly important life lesson my children would miss if they never learned to properly tuck in a sheet? What character trait were they lacking from the absence of a bed making chore? (And then the dreaded question—*Were we failing as parents???*) How wonderful it was to embrace the truth that making beds is a Grey area. Now, I am no longer distressed when I read other people's bed making opinions and recommendations, because I know He will lead our family in it if it becomes His will for us someday. I can rest assured, knowing that His unique plans for my family are *always* best. If there is something God has called you to that you are struggling with, I encourage you to surrender and find rest in His best for you.

Surrendering to God's best brings rest!

My friend Crystal and I were talking about something that we just weren't getting around to doing. She concluded that it was "a good idea—*for someone else!*"

Jesus Is the Pattern

Realizing that His will for families (in regard to the Grey areas of life) will look different from family to family, we are freed to appreciate these differences, instead of looking to others as the standard of what a godly family looks like. (It is important to note that we should all be seeking to be godly examples "in speech, in conduct, in love, in faith, in purity" [I Timothy 4:12], and should absolutely look to those who are such an example in our lives. What I am referring to here is thinking every single aspect of someone's life is the standard for Christian living.) As the Lord leads us in our unique family culture, we can happily learn from other people and also be protected from the danger of seeking to validate our own decisions by finding problems with others. I cannot even begin to tell you how incredibly freeing it has been to stop evaluating practically everyone and everything, trying to discover the right or best way to do things! Is it really my business how God is uniquely leading you, and vice versa? Of course, He may put something on our heart to pray for someone, and He might lead us to approach a sister in love over something of concern (or the other way around). He may also use someone as an example for us to emulate in a particular area, but these kinds of body ministry are a far cry from looking for the standard amongst the flock. Jesus alone is our Standard and, within the parameters He has set for us in His Word, there is much room for differences.

This bears repeating, sisters—

there is much room for differences!

Karin Kyle, who is married to Pastor Damien Kyle of Calvary Chapel, Modesto, gave a good illustration of this in a teaching at a women's conference. She shared how in one of her Bible Study classes she had handed out a dress pattern to each of the ladies. They were given the assignment to take it home and, following the pattern, make a dress out of any material that they wanted. She said that at the end of the class, when all of the completed dresses were brought back, it was amazing to see how different they looked even though they had been cut from the same pattern. In the same way, Jesus is our Pattern. Yes, we are to pattern ourselves after Him, but, within the parameters of His example, we are allowed distinctions—distinctions that reflect the creativity of our God.

Made with Love

We readily teach our children that they are God's unique and precious creation, and yet can so easily forget the same truths apply to us, as well:

> For you formed my inward parts;
> you knitted me together
> in my mother's womb.
> I praise you, for I am
> *fearfully and wonderfully made.*
> Wonderful are your works;
> my soul knows it very well.
> –Psalm 139:13, 14
> (emphasis mine)

I think many comparisons would disappear in the body of Christ if we all could truly grasp our worth from God's perspective. (To be clear, none of us are worthy to be called His children—yet look at the price He paid to redeem us! In His great grace and everlasting love, He considered a relationship with us–*we who were His enemies*– worth going to the cross.) There is room in His heart and plan for us all; every part is important and every person is valuable! I love the saying "We're all His favorites." This reminds me of a time when Elijah asked Mickey if he was his "favorite son." Mickey reminded him that, since Zeke had been born, he now had two great sons. Elijah was not satisfied with that answer and asked, "But what about 'favorite?' What about *that word*?" I think he needed to be reassured that the addition of a little brother had in no way diminished his father's love for him. It hadn't, of course, and it is the same with our Heavenly Father. When you are tempted to feel "less than" in the family of God, please remember that we are all His favorites. We are different by design, so no more comparing, sisters! Let's just follow the Leader and let Him make us what He wants us to be. *He does all things well* (Mark 7:37)!

Appreciating others' gifts brings joy:

Esther (~ 7) said admiringly, "One day Eva drew the most *'flabulous'* anteater . . ."

When reading, instead of comparing ourselves with the author, we can appreciate the woman God has created her to be, while keeping an open heart to anything in her example that He may be calling us to emulate. Regretfully, I went through a rather long and lonely season where I couldn't receive much of anything from anyone. How much I missed out on! Our personalities, wisdom, natural abilities, spiritual giftings, and unique perspectives can add so much to each other's lives. We should run *toward* one other, not away. We need each other, sisters, so "let us consider how to stir up one another to love and good works, not neglecting to meet together, as is the habit of some, but encouraging one another, and all the more as you see the Day drawing near" (Hebrews 10:24, 25).

As you read, let Him lead:

You may not struggle as I did in regard to books, however, I believe we should all be sensitive to the Spirit when making reading choices. I must confess this exhortation hits super, super, *super* close to home for me, because I love, love, *love* to read on the Internet, where everything is so short and succinct. I can skim through a dozen different articles on a dozen different topics in less than half an hour, and it is something I gravitate to as a mental escape. Unfortunately, I have frequently squandered time online when I knew God wanted me doing something else. There have also been many times that I read things I shouldn't have, so this next section is written with a number of fingers pointing back at me:

My friend Page said, "Just because you could, doesn't mean you should." Or, as 1 Corinthians 6:12 says, not everything "lawful" is "helpful." We live in a unique period of history where a vast array of teachings, ideas, and opinions are at our fingertips. We may find ourselves clicking on article after article without giving much thought to the fact that it takes time to read and process a lot of information—*time that God may not be giving us.* And, if needed, will there be time to be a Berean to make sure that what we are reading is in accordance with sound doctrine?

Again, books and articles can be very helpful resources, and what is not good for one, may be just what God has for another (different dresses, same Pattern, right?). My heart in writing this is simply to encourage all of us to involve God in our reading choices. After all, we "are not [our] own" (1 Corinthians 6:19)—*we are His.*

Know that the LORD, he is God!
It is he who made us, and we are his;
we are his people, and the sheep of his pasture.
—Psalm 100:3

Ela Ellis

CHAPTER 5
Shadow of the Supermom

**Eden (6), trying to convince us that she
was ready to move up a grade in Sunday school, said,
"They just teach me what I already know."
Continuing to make her argument,
she told us that whenever they asked who built the ark,
she already knew the answer—
*"Moses!"***

Have you ever found yourself measuring yourself up against a standard that does not even exist? From all I had read over the years, a picture of an ideal woman had formed in my imagination. It looked something like this: she rose when the rooster crowed and always looked well put-together; made homemade bread out of exotic grains that she never forgot about in the oven and subsequently burned; churned butter from the raw milk she milked from her dairy cow early each morning; sewed her own lovely clothing, tablecloths, and curtains; maintained sparkling clean windows and glistening floors; had children with impeccable manners and, of course, perpetually clean fingernails, while she excelled at small talk and all things social. A little exaggeration there, but I did live under a similar mental shadow.

Elijah (~10) was working hard on a Mother's Day card for quite a while. I was so touched . . . *until I learned it was for our dog!*

(Now I may not be a supermom, and there was that one difficult season I went through that lasted, oh, about ten years, but . . . *really?*)

But what about Proverbs 31? It isn't just a terrifying figment of someone's imagination, but a Biblical example of godly womanhood. This passage of Scripture intimidated me *for years,* and I used to wonder things like the following:

Are we supposed to sew our own clothing (v. 13)?
Does the fact that she clothes herself in "fine linen and purple" (v. 22) mean God is commanding us to be extremely well-dressed and to always wear purple?

One rainy day, I asked Elijah (3) if he wanted to go down to the mailbox. He said, "No . . . *it's purple out there!"*

Does driving the thirty minutes it takes me to get to Sam's Club count as bringing "food from afar" (v.14)?
Are we supposed to wash and fold laundry until the wee hours of the morning so that our lamp "does not go out at night" (v. 18)? Does the verse that says "she rises while it is yet night" (v. 15) mean we have to get up before the sun rises? *(And are these two verses combined saying we are supposed to get very little sleep!?)*
These are all questions I have asked myself and most likely cried tears over. I included the story about Eden at the beginning of this chapter because it is a great illustration of getting the Bible wrong, which is what I was doing with Proverbs 31. Thankfully, I am learning how to rightly study the Word of God, and it has really helped me out

with this passage. Knowing what type of literary genre (writing style) you are studying can be essential to correct Bible interpretation. My pastor, Nick Triveri, said literary style is "like the packaging in which God sends His Word." The literary styles of the Bible can be categorized as Historical Narrative, Didactic (Teaching), Poetry, Prophecy, Parable, and Wisdom Literature. Historical Narratives are descriptions of events that happened in the past; Didactic Literature involves doctrine and instructions regarding right living; the book of Psalms is an example of Poetry in the Bible; Prophetic Literature describes future events; Parables are the stories Jesus told that illustrated some of His teachings; and the book of Proverbs is the Bible's main piece of Wisdom Literature.

In its introduction to Proverbs, the ESV Study Bible says, "Proverbs often seem to be mere observations about life, but their deeper meanings will reveal themselves if the following grid is applied: (1) What *virtue* does this proverb commend? (2) What *vice* does it hold up for disapproval? (3) What *value* does it affirm?"[15] (I would add it is a good habit to pray before we read the Word and ask God to give us understanding.) Concerning the Proverbs 31 woman, a note in the ESV Study Bible says:

> This lofty portrait of excellence sets such a high standard that it can be depressing to godly women today until its purpose is understood. First, the woman embodies in all areas of life the full character of wisdom commended throughout this book.... as with other character types, this profile is an *ideal*: a particular example of full-scale virtue and wisdom toward which the faithful are willing to be molded . . . It is not expected that any one woman will look exactly like this in every respect.[16]

---

[15] Taken from the ESV® Study Bible (The Holy Bible, English Standard Version®), copyright ©2008 by Crossway, a publishing ministry of Good News Publishers. Used by permission. All rights reserved.
[16] Ibid.

In thinking that God was giving me my daily To-Do list with these thirty-one verses, I was totally missing the point. Proverbs 31 is not a list of specific things that God is commanding us to do (hold a spindle, wear purple, buy a field)—it is a poetic description of a virtuous woman. I was missing "the forest for the trees." The bigger picture is behind the examples—it is the principles that transcend time, culture, and situation. This chapter is far less intimidating to me now that I know to look at the principles behind the examples. I can actually read it now without having a meltdown!

Eva (4) was throwing a fit because her makeshift tent kept falling apart. I corrected her a couple of times before she came over to me with her hands on her hips and asked, "What would you do if your tent kept falling down? *What would you do!?*"

God isn't commanding all of us to make clothing out of raw materials, like wool and flax (v. 13), but, rather, showing that a godly woman values and embraces hard work in order to care for the physical needs of her family: she "looks well to the ways of her household" (v. 27). Clearly, this verse cannot literally apply to many of us since spinning wool and weaving cloth are not even necessary tasks anymore in much of the world. (Hurrah for progress!)

As for the verse that says she clothes herself in fine linen and purple, I honestly don't know exactly what is being said here, but I do know what it is *not* saying—we aren't being commanded to wear high-end clothing! (And it isn't wrong to wear colors other than purple, or to avoid purple altogether if it is a color you don't particularly like wearing.) A possible interpretation is that since this manner of dressing was the apparel of royalty and the very wealthy, the Proverbs 31 woman, who was clearly of a higher social status, dressed in an appropriate manner for her station in life. As daughters of the King, we too should clothe ourselves appropriately for the high calling we have been given. In 1 Timothy 2:9 and 10,

God tells us how to do so: ". . . women should adorn themselves in respectable apparel, with modesty and self-control, not with braided hair and gold or pearls or costly attire, but with what is proper for women who profess godliness—with good works." And 1 Peter 3:3 and 4 says, "Do not let your adorning be external—the braiding of hair and the putting on of gold jewelry, or the clothing you wear— but let your adorning be the hidden person of the heart with the imperishable beauty of a gentle and quiet spirit, which in God's sight is very precious."

A note in the ESV Study Bible (for 1 Peter 3:3 and 4) says:

> Such "external . . . adorning" can be witnessed in portraits and sculptures from the first century, where the elaborate **braiding of** women's **hair** and the wearing of ostentatious **jewelry** was common in upper-class Roman society. In contrast to this, the Christian woman should focus on inner **(hidden)** beauty **of the heart**. What matters to God is the godly character of the wife, characterized by a **gentle and quiet spirit**. It is clear that Peter is not literally prohibiting all braiding of hair or all wearing of gold jewelry, because if this were the case the same prohibition would apply also to wearing clothing![17]

Using Scripture (New Testament passages) to interpret Scripture (Proverbs 31), we see that there is nothing wrong with dressing nicely (in a modest and tasteful manner), but that our focus needs to be on the true beauty that comes from within. No matter the state of our finances, we can seek to dress in a way that brings glory to our King and rightly represents Him to the world. (P.S. There is not just one right way to do so . . . more about this in Chapter Ten.)

---

[17] Taken from the ESV® Study Bible (The Holy Bible, English Standard Version®), copyright ©2008 by Crossway, a publishing ministry of Good News Publishers. Used by permission. All rights reserved.

And food purchased an hour away is not godlier than what can be bought in the local supermarket. I believe the principle behind verse 14 ("food from afar") is that she cares about what she puts before her family and makes great efforts to provide for their needs. In essence, she loves them through self-sacrificing service.

All for Jesus

Okay, but what about the fact that she is commended for being an excellent wife (v. 10) and for having done excellently (v. 29)? This caused me just as much angst as the details of her industry did! To my legalistic mind, being excellent meant performing at top level in every area. It meant being "my best" (physically, mentally, and emotionally) in every situation and at all times. The problem was, how could I know I was doing my best? Hard work is good, of course, but how hard? If I was encouraged to reach high, how high? If love is the goal, then what is most loving? Certainly, it is loving to change your child's diapers, but were disposable diapers okay, or was I supposed to switch to cloth? If so, then should the cloth be organic cotton? Or is it the best thing to just potty-train your infants (which may work for others, but is not something I have ever been called to)? This is just one example of my tendency to go to the extreme when wondering how I was supposed to do things. On and on *and on* I would go, over just about anything . . . But please don't think for a moment that I was actually trying to do all of the things my legalistic mind came up with! Mostly, I just stewed over them.

I was changing baby Eden's diaper and Zeke (3), meaning to say "disgusting," got his adjectives mixed up and kept saying emphatically, "That is a *gorgeous* poop! That is a *gorgeous* poop!"

Does God really want us pushing ourselves to the nth degree? He does tell us, whatever we do, to "work heartily, as for the Lord" (Colossians 3:23). I now know that working with all of our heart for the Lord doesn't mean pushing ourselves to the utmost at all times, but, instead, means to be completely devoted to Him and surrendered to His will—embracing whatever He has called us to do and serving Him in the moment with an undivided heart. This *is* giving Him our all, but in a wholehearted kind of way, as opposed to the extreme way I had assumed "all" to mean. Working with all of my heart does not mean I *have to* serve three-course meals, train to run a mile in eight minutes, or scrub until I can see my reflection in my kitchen floor. (Unless God leads me in it, of course.)

Remember the goal? *Everything* we do is to be done in love (I Corinthians 16:14). God also tells us what love is. And love is not defined as being as talented, fit, or industrious as possible, but as being kind, patient, forgiving, etc. When I make love the goal, and let God's Word and His Spirit lead me in what love looks like in each particular situation, my yoke becomes easy and my burden light. In the words of one of my favorite *philo*sophers, Phil Robertson, "happy, happy, happy"[18] is the state of being yoked to Christ. I don't mean it is sunshine and flowers all the time—I would define happiness in the Christian life as being blessed in Christ.

I was reading *The Poky Little Puppy*[19] to Zeke. When I read the sentence that says he was "happy as a lark," Zeke asked me, "How happy is a lark?" "So happy," I answered. Then Eva showed up and, *of course*, we had to start all over. When we got to the part about the lark, Zeke informed her with an authoritative air, "Eva, a lark is *soooooo happy!*"

[18] Robertson, Phil. *Happy, Happy, Happy: My Life and Legacy as the Duck Commander.* New York: Howard Books, 2015.
[19] Lowrey, Janette Sebring and Gustaf Tenggren. The Poky Little Puppy. New York City: Golden Books, 2001.

Laura Ellis

"You Have a Book, Laura—Read It!"
(My mom would often tell me this during
my intense struggle with legalism.)

My trouble with legalism came not just from reading too many books with too little discernment, but in neglecting the most important Book far too often. I was not filling myself with the _full_ counsel of God's Word, so it was easy for me to take things out of context and interpret them apart from the big Biblical picture. Over and over, the New Testament points out the diversity of people in the body of Christ in regard to giftings, callings, and situations. And, of course, the Bible was written for people from many time periods and different cultures, where the details of everyday life can vary greatly. Therefore, Proverbs 31 cannot be painting a literal one-size-fits-all portrait! Again, it is a beautiful and inspiring example of a virtuous woman in Biblical days meant to teach principles that transcend time, culture, and situation.

I once asked my friend Terry, a mature sister in the Lord, if feeling like she could never measure up to the Proverbs 31 woman had ever been an issue for her. She said it hadn't been—she knew there was nothing good in her apart from Christ, and that He was making her into a unique, beautiful creation in His time. How simple! She was not constantly evaluating every aspect of her life, as I was. She was simply walking humbly with the Lord, and trusting Him to make her into the virtuous woman that He wanted her to be.

I'm so thankful God gives His "students" time to grow:

After Zeke (10) had taught his younger siblings something, I overheard him telling them that they needed to "write an essay" on what they had just learned. _(Two of them didn't even know their ABCs yet!)_

60

Proverbs 31 is not meant to condemn or burden us daughters of the King; rather, it is meant to inspire us to be hardworking servants in our home, and in our various spheres of influence, as the Lord leads us in the particulars. Having read it, we should come away wanting to be a woman of virtue also: a woman whose husband's heart "trusts in her" (v. 11), whose children one day "rise up and call her blessed" (v. 28), and who values the true beauty that comes from the fear of the Lord (v.30).

Now, when I read about the Proverbs 31 woman, I am inspired to serve even more in the ways God has called me to—instead of worrying about how I am supposed to buy a field and plant a vineyard! I can help our finances in many ways without feeling as if I have to take on an Internet "cottage industry." Honestly, right now, I'm just trying to stop overspending every time I go to Wal-Mart . . . and that's a good start for me!

Ministry in Wal-Mart at midnight:

Okay, so it is earlier than midnight, but definitely on the later end, when I have been known to go shopping at our local Wal-Mart. The store is sparsely populated at that time, and I can casually stroll along with my cart without getting stuck in a traffic jam of other carts. It certainly isn't for everyone, but I enjoy it. However, I used to wonder if I was missing the mark by being out so late. Was it a sin that I didn't plan my shopping well enough so as to avoid any last-minute trips to the store at night? But after a number of clear "God appointments" in the late-night aisles of Wal-Mart, the Lord set me free from those legalistic thoughts. Later, it was even further confirmation when Ezekiel (9) said the following in his nighttime prayer: "I pray that mom's ministry in Wal-Mart would grow." I was reminded that God wants His light shining all over the place . . . day *and* night!

CHAPTER 6

When God Guides, He Provides

This is God
our God forever and ever.
He will guide us forever.
–Psalm 48:14

"**A**re all these yours?"
"Wow, your hands are full!"
"*You are brave.*"

These are the kinds of comments I frequently hear when I take some, *or rarely all*, of my children out. I have even heard the "You do know how this happens, don't you?" (Got to love the embarrassing questions total strangers will ask you in the aisle of the grocery store . . .)

Eva (~18 months) really enjoyed socializing at the grocery store. *Much to my dismay,* she liked to shout "Hi guys!" across the store to other shoppers. (Of course, if she wasn't *my* child, I would have thought it was super cute . . . pride is such a joy stealer!)

Parenting a large number of children is something that is looked upon as strange by many in our culture. Driving around with your family in one of those white monstrosities they call a fifteen-passenger van isn't exactly the norm. We have one such behemoth, and I attract even more attention to us by all the curbs I roll over. (It has been good for my fear of man, though—God really does have a sense of humor!)

Large-family living often challenges many of the ways things are done in our western society, but cultural norms (unless also God's laws, of course) are not moral principles. There are many cultural norms that are simply people's preferences and personal standards of living. We can take widely accepted beliefs and strongly held opinions concerning children and child rearing (like, "parents can't give enough attention, opportunities, or protection to more than two children") and make them laws in our own lives. Legalism does not have to originate within the church.

I heard this idea for a "Family Psalm" presented by Gisela Yohannan:

Using Psalm 136, which tells of Israel's history and God's love and faithfulness toward them, she showed us how to construct our own psalm by listing (chronologically, if possible) the events in our lives that stand out like signposts of God's love and faithfulness. She encouraged us to end each entry with the phrase that repeats over and over again in Psalm 136: "for his steadfast love endures forever."

"Come Lay with Me a Lil' Bit"
(something three-year-old Zeke would often say when I put him down for bed)

A frequent criticism of parents with many children is that they do not have enough time to spend with each of them. I have learned that while we cannot give our kids the same amount of attention that a parent with one or two children is able to give, the Lord *will* give us the time with each one that He wants us to have, as we seek Him for direction. One way we have been led to make special time is by taking a couple of kids with us when we run errands, go to appointments, and attend various social functions. Our doctor has gotten used to there usually being three or more of us crowded into the room when someone has an appointment. (Although, there are times I wish I had gone alone—like when Elijah overheard the nurse tell me my weight and then could not stop bringing it up afterwards. This really was my fault . . . Why I didn't consider the temptation such information would pose to a teenage boy escapes me. Despite being in my sixteenth year of parenting, I still make plenty of rookie mistakes.) There are also those spontaneous moments that God provides for us to connect with them (read a book, play a game, have a talk). Much death to self is required for me here (and I have, regrettably, missed innumerable opportunities), but the more I die to myself, the more I am "surprised by joy." (This is taken from the title of C.S. Lewis' book[20] about his conversion to Christ. God's goodness just continues to surprise us as we follow Him!)

I asked Zeke (2) whether he wanted Mommy or Daddy. He thought for a minute and then, with a big grin, shouted the names of his aunt and uncle. *(Schooled by a toddler!)*

Life Is Not Fair

Some people seem to have great concern that it is not fair for older children in large families to help raise their younger siblings. If by "raise," they mean assisting toddlers with tasks like putting on shoes and getting into car seats, then we are guilty of this. It may not be fair in the sense that other children in smaller families do not have to fill Sippy cups for little ones, but to quote mothers everywhere: "Life is not fair!" God has called

---

[20] Lewis, C.S. *Surprised by Joy: The Shape of My Early Life 1st Edition.* New York City: Harcourt, Brace, Jovanovich, 1966.

our children to be in a large family, and when we are seeking to have Him structure the workings of our home, whatever extra work they have is part of His will for them. While we certainly want them to have a childhood full of fun and discovery, we also know that learning to serve and care for other's interests (Philippians 2:4) is equally as important.

I asked Elijah (8) to do too much and he said, "I don't want to be disrespectful, but I'm not an octopus!" He got it from me. I can't remember where I got it from, but it is a good thing for us moms to remember . . . *and occasionally remind other people of.*

I May Not Know What the Future Holds, but I Know Who Holds the Future!

I sometimes have terrible nightmares where something catastrophic is happening and I can't rescue all of my children because there are just too many of them. It is generally more challenging to keep track of a lot of kids; knowing this, has only served to heighten the fears I already struggle with as a mom. If I lose track of one of my children, especially one of the younger ones, I usually go from zero to full-on PANIC mode in seconds. *Literally, seconds.* Remember when I said the 9-1-1 operator asked if she could send out an ambulance for me after I found Zeke? It's that bad. I honestly believe there are some people at my church who think a terrified look is my regular face. I've been known to push people out of my way when I'm looking for one of my children, and my neighbor even called the police once because I was screaming in my driveway when I hadn't been able to find my toddler after looking for a *very short* amount of time.

When I asked Ezra (2) how he knew mommy loved him, he yelled, "Ahhhhhhh!" I asked him again, and he gave the same response. I then realized it was his impersonation of me yelling whenever I look for him.

I can do my best to keep my eyes on my kids, but there are no guarantees except for this one: God is in control. ("He's Got the Whole World in His Hands" is a good song for moms too!) One night, Esther asked if she could take our dog outside to go the bathroom. We had let her do so by herself before, but I had a check in my spirit about it on this particular evening. I asked Mickey to send Eva with her. They were instructed to go only as far as the porch, and to just watch the dog from there. Praise God for the lack of peace He gave me— a mountain lion attacked our dog next to the side of our house (she miraculously survived with minimal injury). The mountain lion then came to around ten feet from our front door—thankfully, the girls had already run back inside. No, I may not have been able to protect my children in that situation, but God did. And even if that night had resulted in tragedy, He would still have been in control, and He would still have been good. We may not understand why He allows some things to happen, but we can always cling to His goodness.

Playing Mountain Lion was all the rage in our house for a season. So was Running-like-a-Cheetah . . . which was played *exactly* like it sounds.

Me Time

God provides the time that He wants me to have. I have had to let go of many expectations, which has *not* been easy, but I am learning that our Good Shepherd takes care of His sheep! Not only has He provided regular breaks for me (and yes, I have been known to practically run out the door to that glorious experience of a quiet drive in an empty vehicle with no seat belt issues), but I have also found myself lying down in green pastures and resting beside still waters (Psalm 23:2) when I least expected it, and often in ways I would not have expected. (Isn't it amazing what an oasis a toothpaste-smeared bathroom can be?) While getting time to myself is definitely a blessing, I also know that it is God Who restores my soul (Psalm 23:3). And this is something no amount of "me time" could ever do.

Some bathroom humor:

*Not being the most consistent leg shaver, I finally got around to it one day. Later, Elijah (~12) stormed out of the bathroom wanting to know who had *"bathed the cat!"* in there.

*One of my sons, not knowing anything about feminine products, found the basket that held my personal items and made a "craft" out of them for me.

Cheaper by the (Half) Dozen

I have heard people ask how large families can afford to live. Things are certainly tighter with more bodies to clothe and more mouths to feed (of course, what is considered constrained finances to one family may be extravagant living to another), but our God clothes the lilies of the field and feeds the birds of the air (Matthew 6:26–30), so we know that He will also continue to provide all that we need. In a culture that offers a multitude of wants, we may have to learn to be content (Philippians 4:11–13), but "godliness with contentment is great gain" (1 Timothy 6:6)! As the song says, if we "turn [our] eyes upon Jesus . . . the things of earth will grow strangely dim, in the light of His glory and grace."

Something that has been helpful to me is learning that family fun doesn't have to be expensive. Besides the usual (board games, family walks, picnics in the park), here is a list of ten cheap *(or free!)* group activities:

1. **Dance Contest**—Have everybody pick out a favorite song and show off their epic moves.
2. **Plays and Talent Shows**—It is a good idea to record these, if possible, because it will be a source of great entertainment years later!
3. **Paper Airplanes and Aluminum Foil Boat Contests**—You can Google "paper airplane designs" and find countless directions— from ones that are easy for children to make, to designs that you practically need a degree in aerospace engineering in order to follow. With the planes, you can compete to see whose flies the straightest, farthest, or fastest. And with the boats, you can see which one will float the longest or carry the most items.
4. **Frisbee Golf**—Some parks have courses open to the public for free. You can also make a course in your yard or down a road by just aiming at specific targets.
5. **Full Moon Drive**—Have everyone get in the car (in their jammies), bring a treat to share, and drive somewhere the moon is visible.
6. **Water Gun War**—You can have two teams compete to see who can be the first to take down the other team's piece of bread (hanging from a tree or rooftop by a string).
7. **Hide & Seek**—As long as someone doesn't get scared, it can be fun playing this in the dark with flashlights.
8. **Old Fashioned Pillow Fight**—Our kids like to prep beforehand by building up their arsenal of pillows and making forts to hide behind.
9. **Potato Sack Races**—We've used pillow cases and thick garbage bags at different times. It is best to play on large grassy fields.
10) **Scavenger Hunt**—These are especially fun to play with hidden birthday gifts!

11) **Cooking Competition**—This is a great way to use up a lot of food that needs to get eaten ASAP. Put it all out and see who can make the best dish.

12) **Twenty Questions**—Since I tell my children "hate is too strong a word" (for non-evil things), I will just say that I deeply, deeply, *deeply* dislike this game, but it is free and involves everybody so I've included it.

Another great family-time idea I came across is "Vacation at Home." First, pick a day on your schedule where you don't have anything planned. Next, so no one has to cook, purchase convenience food that you don't normally buy and that your kids frequently request. Then, pick some fun at-home activities (like, homemade slip 'n slides made with tarps, a movie marathon, *or absolutely nothing at all*). Use paper plates, give everybody the day off from chores and school work, and just enjoy being together.

Seven Kids x Two Feet = a Lot of Footprints

Now this one I have never had trouble with, but I know there are those who wonder how, with so many children, we can justify our "carbon footprint" on the environment. While we definitely want to be good stewards of God's creation, and should try to live responsibly per His leading, we also know He gave us these children to raise to know and love Him. Is a reduced "greenhouse effect" more important than eternal beings made in His image with the potential to glorify Him with their lives and worship Him for all of eternity? *I don't think so!* Besides, Jesus is coming back to make all things new (Revelation 21:5). Honestly, the only footprints I am concerned about my kids making are their spiritual ones as they walk through this life. (Okay, and maybe the muddy ones tracked in on my newly mopped floors). The cry of my heart is that they will be led by the Lord all the days of their lives until He takes them home to be with Him in glory.

"For behold, I create new heavens
and a new earth,
and the former things shall not be remembered
or come into mind."
-Isaiah 65:17

"Our God Is a Blessing God"
-Pastor Nick Triveri

Elijah (3) was talking to his grandma in Wisconsin. When he got off the phone, he said, *"Boy, that grandma has a lot of cats!"*

People often ask me, "How do you do it?" And I frequently reply, "I don't know!" It may not feel possible at times, but our God is in the business of doing the impossible (Matthew 19:26), through the weak, in His strength: " 'Not by might, nor by power, but by my Spirit, says the LORD of hosts' " (Zechariah 4:6). And as much as I have struggled being a "mother of many," I can say with all of my heart that it is a blessing, because *they truly are a blessing.* It is also a blessing because it is what God has called me to and His plans for us are always best. (He knew I needed some tall fences in my life!) As Psalm 119:68 says, He is good, and what He does is good.

So, in answer to the frequent grocery store questions:

"Yes, they are all mine."
"Yes, my hands are full!"
But "No, I'm not brave—

just blessed!"

You know you have a big family when:
(all of these things are taken from my life)

- you purchase back-to-school supplies for your children and the cashier asks if you are a school teacher
- you take up an entire row of seats at church
- there are two couches and two love seats in your living room so everyone can have a place to sit during movies (and someone still often ends up on the floor!)
- you have to make a rule about how many children can be on the trampoline at a time (and then you end up purchasing a second one anyway)
- your family vehicle is referred to as "The Bus"
- a date night means you "only" have one or two of the little ones with you
- leaving social functions looks and feels like herding cats
- signing everyone's name on cards takes too much time so you just sign "The _____ Clan"
- you go to get flu vaccines and they run out before everyone gets one
- you buy Band-Aids in bulk and find the wrappers *everywhere*—even in the fridge!
- a bunch of bananas is just an afternoon snack
- even making convenience food takes time because you have to open so many packages
- your "coat wall" looks like the entry hall in a kindergarten classroom
- you run through several names before you get to the name of the child you are trying to address
- your neighbor tells you he thought you ran an in-home day care when he first moved in
- you put on a play of the nativity and have nearly every part filled
- when out as a family, people tend to turn into bobbleheads as you pass by because they are counting all of your children
- you find yourself Googling "big family" in your free time—just to be reminded that there are others with lists like this one!

CHAPTER 7
Free to Be Me!

**Playing some kind of imaginary
game with paper crowns, Elijah (4) said,
"I am the King. Esther is the Queen. And Eva . . ."
He paused, thinking for a moment,
and then announced:
"You're the Jack!"**

These next four chapters share about some specific areas in my life where I used to struggle as to what was *the way* to do things. As I have already shared, the Lord has freed me from standards that He had not given me. He's also led me in some ways that were quite different from what I had previously either thought or been taught were the best way to do things.

I hope this glimpse into my (sometimes unconventional) life encourages those who are struggling with legalism to trust the Lord to lead them in creating their unique family culture. I can still remember how relieved I was when I read about a Christian mother who did not serve meals at regular times and would let her children eat their dessert first. The relief I felt wasn't because I was being led in a similar way; it was simply because I saw an example of a godly family doing things differently than I was familiar with—and it was okay! (Queens and Jacks may be different, but they are still part of the same royal suite.)

It is important to note that most of the things I am writing about pertain to those of us who are blessed to live a lifestyle where what we eat, how we clean, the ways we decorate, and the methods in which we educate our children *are even issues at all!* Many people just try to fill their stomachs, stay clothed, and have a warm place to sleep. This is a sobering thought, and something I think many of us need to be reminded of often. May we never lose sight of the fact that just having food on the table, clothes in our closets, and a roof over our heads is a tremendous blessing!

---

*My kids once ran a lemonade stand at our church to raise money for a camel (a mission group was supplying camels to poor families overseas as a source of income). Elijah (~10) prayed for his camel to have two humps, while Eva's (~8) prayer was far more practical—she prayed that the camel wouldn't have "bad breath."

*This must have been an area of concern for her because another time she asked, "Does camel breath smell bad?" *(I would assume . . .)*

CHAPTER 8
Making Peace with Ramen Noodles

**Not wanting to finish her dinner,
but still desiring dessert, Esther (~7) said,
"My healthy side is full, but my treat side isn't!"**

There was a time, or I should say there have been *many times*, when God convicted me about us eating too much junk food and eating out too often. (And about giving my toddler and myself too many chocolate chips to get through "a moment," thus creating an insatiable treat craving due to a high volume of moments . . . Moderation is a lesson I have had to be taught *repeatedly*.) Making healthier, homemade meals is something God has definitely led me in before, but there was a season when I became overly focused on things needing to be made from scratch. How the pendulum has swung to and fro in my life! I started thinking it was wrong to use convenience foods like Top Ramen. Of course, packaged items are not usually as healthy as homemade meals, but there is no command in Scripture to serve the healthiest, homiest food possible. And there are times convenience food can be a serious help!

When this dawned on me, it was like a huge emotional breath of fresh air and sigh of relief all at the same time. It reminded me of when I was freed from feeling as if everything I bought had to be organic. The larger our family got, the more expensive it became to buy organic food, and I came to the realization that, for the most part, it just wasn't for us anymore. I learned that I can pray for wisdom regarding food choices and trust God to lead us as we eat. Ultimately, He has written our days (Psalm 139:16), and that truth brings me much comfort whenever I get overwhelmed by all of the diet recommendations out there. If you followed all of them, you could end up only eating raw seaweed and drinking distilled water, with a kitchen counter overrun with vitamins and other supplements . . . *no thanks, I'm good!*

Once, Mickey came home from work and the kids started sniffing his shirt like crazed puppies, insisting he had eaten ice cream that day—he had!

Please know, I am *not* trying to write an Organic vs. Nonorganic or Homemade vs. Convenience Food chapter here. Certainly, there may be those who are led to eat all organic or serve only homemade meals. There are also those who need to cut out certain foods due to health issues, personal preferences, and other reasons. (For example, due to a caffeine sensitivity, I felt led to stop eating chocolate— which wasn't an easy transition since it was a major food group in my diet!) But healthy eating is subjective and definitely a Grey area. For some, "healthy" means drinking fresh goat milk and eating raw cheese from their own backyard farm. For others, it means eating less fast-food and choosing water over soda. I have been among the latter, and know God may call me to the former. (In fact, my kids fervently prayed for goats for quite a while.) My heart is simply to share how I was set free from a standard that God had not given me.

I once read in a book the recommendation that children should be served the same breakfast and lunch on most days. I also read somewhere else that kids should not be given condiments for their food. These were both books written for Christians, and the restrictions were given, at least from my perspective, as if there were spiritual reasons connected to them. Comments like that would have given me much trouble in the past, but now, by God's grace, I can see they are just opinions.

Colossians 2:20–23 says:

> If with Christ you died to the elemental spirits
> of the world, why, as if you were still alive in the
> world, do you submit to regulations—"Do not
> handle, Do not taste, Do not touch" (referring to
> things that all perish as they are used)—according
> to human precepts and teachings? These have
> indeed an appearance of wisdom in promoting
> self-made religion and asceticism and severity to
> the body, but they are of no value in stopping the
> indulgence of the flesh.

So, if you ever come across a teaching that says it is wrong for
your kids to eat ketchup with their fries or ranch with their carrots
(perish the thought!), please read this passage of Scripture again,
and trust God to lead you personally in your family's food choices.

Elijah (~8) asked me what relish was made of. I told him pickles. He was
surprised (and probably pretty relieved) and said, "It isn't made up of
ground-up frogs? *I wondered why Mema ate it!*"

Food is a part of life, but " 'life is more than food' " (Luke 12:23).
In thinking some foods were godlier than others, and that I was a
better wife, mom, and Christian the more "godly meals" I served
my family, I had made food something it never should have been.
I was so blessed by what one mom wrote regarding the blessing of
cold cereal for busy mamas. How refreshing to read that after all
of the "Cereal is bad!" and "Don't feed that sugared cardboard to
your kids!" opinions I had read previously. I am also glad to know
that I am free to serve Top Ramen. I now have a large flat of it in my
cupboard that brings me great joy! (Not only because it is helpful,
but because it is also a reminder of my freedom from legalism.)

My favorite breakfast recipe:

Cold Cereal
Prep Time: fifteen seconds

Cereal

1. Pour cereal into a bowl.
2. Add milk or yogurt (or just eat like trail mix).

"What's for Dinner?"

Another area in which I battled legalism was over meal planning. How I felt like a failure because most of my dinner-cooking experience was looking at the clock around 4:30 p.m. and wondering what to make for dinner. Consequently, I have become quite skilled in the "art of the griddle." And no, tacos or grilled cheese are not less godly than a roast chicken with all the trimmings. Love is the goal, not some perfect meal plan! Love your family by feeding them, and let the Lord lead you in the specifics. If He wants you stepping up your game in the kitchen, He will show you.

I have read, and also heard it said, that women should always be learning so as to improve on their homemaking skills. One woman wrote that we need to be continually reading books and articles pertaining to our calling as wives, mothers, and homemakers. Now I'm not saying this a bad idea, and some sisters may certainly be called to do so, but to say this is what all of us ought to be doing is false. What we *are* instructed to grow in continually is "the grace and knowledge of our Lord and Savior Jesus Christ" (2 Peter 3:18). The Lord is the Farmer. He grows us in the ways that *He* sees fit, and as we submit to His work, we will not miss out on any of the good things He has planned for us!

"I like fish tail—tastes just like potato chips!" I didn't write down which one of my children said this, but I have a pretty good guess: I'm thinking it is the one who thinks every part of a rib, except for the bone, is edible. ("Pick your battles" may be a wise saying, but oh, is it hard to put into practice sometimes!)

Because of an increasingly busy season of life, I decided to start incorporating more structure in the food department, but, as I am apt to do, I was soon on information overload searching for the "perfect" system. One day, I was telling my sister Kelsey about yet another meal planning book that I wanted to purchase. She essentially said, "Stop getting books, Laura. You don't need more ideas; you don't need new recipes!" The Lord used what she said to lead me into this simple method: I wrote down approximately twenty meals that I already knew how to make and that most of us like (sorry buddy, majority wins). The goal is to use that list to plan most of our dinners for the month. To help even further simplify my meal planning, I also came up with themes for each day of the week: like, Taco Tuesday (Mexican), Fish Friday (fish and potatoes), and Spaghetti Saturday (Italian). I am still working toward making this a regular part of my life (because it takes me *forever and a day* to implement new processes), but just having a manageable list of meals to work with has made things much easier. Because I am so familiar with the recipes, I automatically stock up on many of the ingredients, which means I usually have what I need for at least several dinners.

Once-a-month cooking used to sound to me about as hard as sentence diagraming in a foreign language, but I eventually realized that instead of approaching it as an "all or nothing" thing, I could narrow it down. After my big shopping trip at Sam's Club, I can cook and prepare *some* things I will use throughout the coming weeks. I might throw a bunch of chicken breasts in the crockpot and then freeze them in meal sized portions; brown ground beef to be used in various recipes; slice onions and peppers for fajitas, and dice them for other dishes; chop carrots and celery for stew; make spaghetti sauce; and prepare a couple of freezer meals. Older children can join in, turning it into a great family activity. My friend Kay did something similar with her children and said, "It seemed easier for the kids to open up and talk with us when they were busy doing something."

Another way the Lord has gently led me in is in regard to meals for ministry. Bringing a homemade meal isn't something that comes easy for me in any shape or form, but, in my orange-chicken-and-cream-cheese-wonton-loving-opinion, Chinese take-out is just as filling and thoughtful. If you also struggle getting a home-cooked meal out the door, take it from someone who has had a lot of meals delivered (due to the delivery of many babies) that a pizza or any other number of take-out dinners is such a blessing.

One of the reasons I should probably avoid homemade meals for ministry:

I once made a meal for a family in our church that had just had a baby. I cooked a stew in my large crockpot and then split it between our two families. After I had delivered their dinner, I found a metal nail floating in the pot as I was serving our dinner. It turns out Zeke (the one and only) had decided it would be a great joke to put two nails in the pot while it was cooking. *(Because isn't that just hilarious?)*

Sometimes "less is more," which is nice to know in this Internet Age of a hundred and one ways to cook asparagus. Please know, I am not trying to dissuade anyone from being creative in the kitchen. (If you are one of those people who never like to cook the same thing twice, please "Google" asparagus recipes to your heart's content!) I'm simply sharing my simple cooking approach to encourage anyone paralyzed by information overload in the food department to take a deep breath, pray, and ask the Lord to bring simplicity into your life. *He will!*

"Mom, I'm Hungry!"

First things first:

Zeke (~ 3) said, "Mom, I'm hungry . . . and I have a wert [wart]."

Here are some unconventional ideas and examples of mothers feeding their children. By "unconventional," I mean it challenges my once-perceived notions of how a godly family was supposed to eat: always around the table, and on lovely ceramic plates featuring a colorful and organic balance of the five-food groups, which had been cooked by mom from scratch. *Please do not get me wrong*, eating together as a family, setting a beautiful table, and serving a homemade meal are all wonderful blessings! They just aren't Biblical commands. I hope the following ideas serve as a reminder that there are many ways to be a good mom. May you be encouraged to seek God's leading as you meet your family's needs.

Breakfast

1) I read of one mom's morning routine where she served her kids breakfast in "courses" (like, a cup of milk, followed by a piece of toast, and then some fruit), while they watched a DVD and she woke up with a cup of coffee.

Elijah (2) spilled a cup of hot tea on himself. "Hot Tea" became a saying he associated with bad things. One day, he was playing basketball with his Aunt Kelsey when the ball hit his leg and he immediately shouted, "HOT TEA!"

2) On a reality television show, a mom of ten children served items from the griddle as they became available. This is such a great idea for things like tacos and pancakes. No, they don't all eat at the same time—*but they all eat!*

3) Have dessert! I enjoy surprising my kids with treats for breakfast from time to time. I have a vague memory of serving ice cream once or twice, but it must have made quite the impression on Eva (4) because she told me that two of her favorite breakfast foods were "'oakmeal' and ice cream." I got the great idea to serve vanilla ice cream *on* oatmeal from author Mary Ostyn. She wrote: "When you think about it, ice cream is mostly cream and sugar, both of which are standard oatmeal toppings. If your kids don't love oatmeal, try a dollop of ice cream on top. They just might change their tune."[21]

4) Make a Bible Breakfast: scatter toaster waffles, drizzled with honey or syrup, all over your living room (face up, of course) and tell your kids to gather their "manna" for the morning. I have only done this a couple of times and they still talk about it like it was the best breakfast *ever.* (And it was just frozen waffles on bed sheets!) If only they were this easy to please all the time . . .

5) Serve cold leftover pizza. It doesn't get any easier.

Lunch

1) We sometimes go to a drive-thru for lunch and then take a mini road-trip, traveling down local roads that we have never driven before. It's such an enjoyable time, with my kids all nicely strapped in their seats *(key point here),* as we experience the adventure of the unknown. (Note: Unless you want a taco bomb

---

[21] Ostyn, Mary. *Family Feasts for $75.00 a Week.* Birmingham: Oxmoor House, 2009. 81.

to go off in the back of your vehicle, I recommend steering clear of hard-shell tacos. They may be cheap, but if time is money, then the amount of time you will spend picking ground beef, shredded cheese, and lettuce shrapnel out of car seats will offset whatever savings you made in the first place.)

Eva (~4), struggling to get buckled in the car, said in such a sorrowful little voice, "Buckle, you are making me *sooooooo sad.*"

---

2) If you have a garden, send your children out with a paring knife (for older children, of course), a cutting board, and a bowl of dressing. Let them pick, dip, and eat to their heart's content. (There is always the hose for washing.)

3) Surprise your kids on a rainy or scorching-hot day with a movie over lunchtime. Pop a big bowl of popcorn, and serve other snack-type (and vacuum-friendly) foods during the show.

4) Take out all of the leftovers in your fridge and let everyone pick what they want to eat. You can also combine complimentary foods together for what I like to refer to as "Skillet Surprise." I recently made a delicious Italian dish by combining leftover pizza (chopped into bite-sized pieces) with some lasagna that needed to be eaten. Skillet Surprise isn't always a *welcome surprise*, however. If you ever throw something together that isn't as good as you had hoped (like the time I added spicy salsa to spaghetti sauce and everyone was super confused and *decidedly unhappy*), you can always put out some kind of treat as an incentive for your kids to eat one small serving.

5) Put out a crockpot of beans, a stack of tortillas, shredded cheese, chopped lettuce, and salsa. Everyone, except for littles, can just serve themselves when they get hungry.

Mickey made lunch one day and Lulu (7) was so surprised that he actually knew how to cook. Ezra (4) said something along the lines of "Of course, Daddy can cook—*he is bigger than Mommy!*"

Snacks

I used to think I wasn't being a good mom if I didn't give my kids a specially prepared snack each day—a mid-afternoon tea would have even been better. Then I just let it go. Now, they can snack on fruit or nuts whenever they get hungry between meals. I don't have to prepare it, and they eat more healthy food this way. *Win, win!*

When Eva (~6) discovered us eating a snack, usually at night, she would say, "If I see it, *I get it!*"

Dinner

1) One mom I read about fed her kids dinner in the bathtub! At first, I admit, I was a little taken aback because I had never heard of such a thing, and then I thought, *Why not?* It would sure save the trouble of wiping down a sauce-covered highchair and everything within two feet of it, picking noodles out of your toddler's sauce-speckled hair, washing sauce out of every crease in her pudgy little hands, and getting around to putting stain remover on her sauce-splattered clothing. (If I have a little one again, I might just try it!) In the summertime, you could also let your kids eat messy barbeque meals outside in their bathing suits, and then just let them run through the sprinkler afterwards.

2) Breakfast for dinner is usually a popular choice. Eggs, pancakes, or yogurt are good options. They say our last meal should actually be the lightest, so this might be just as good for you as it is easy.

3) Have a Fire Pit Roast. I know we want our kids to eat their veggies, but once in a while, a completely synthetic meal of hot dogs and marshmallows is fun; besides, ketchup is technically a fruit product, right?

---

*A paraphrased conversation I had with Zeke when he came home from a camping trip:

Zeke—"We had corndogs!"
Me—"Oh, that is one of my favorites."
Zeke—"Me, too. I love them. You unwrap it."
Me—"You mean the corn part?"
Zeke—"Yeah, you unwrap it and then you get a hotdog!"
Me—"*But that is the best part!*"
Zeke—"No, I don't like it."
(Such a delicacy is clearly wasted on him.)

*Esther (6) asked me, "Are hot dogs 'healfy' without the bun?"
(That would be a no . . .)

---

4) Make a Potato Bar. Cook the potatoes in the oven, crockpot, or microwave, and set out toppings like butter, sour cream, shredded cheese, chili, chives, bacon bits, and steamed broccoli. (You can also do this with mashed potatoes: give everyone a bowlful and let them add their favorite toppings.)

5) Serve rice and beans with fried or scrambled eggs on top. Or just serve rice. Or just beans. This is a good way to give our kids a glimpse of how many other children in the world eat.

Dessert

My "favert" (as Eden would say in her younger years) dessert hack:

Semi-Homemade Peanut Butter Brownies

1 box brownie mix
1/4 cup salted peanut butter

1. Make the batter according to the package instructions.
2. Swirl the peanut butter in.
3. Bake as directed.

Yep, that's it!

I am nowhere near as good at making desserts as I am at eating them, but my Peanut Butter Brownies are foolproof! And yes, it is considered "making it" in my book if you had to open a package, crack open a couple of eggs, wield a wooden spoon, and preheat your oven. As a busy mom, I love using pre-packaged items to help make cooking and baking faster. If you don't have the time (or desire) to make a pie crust from scratch, unwrapping one takes less than a minute! (And, honestly, I think they taste just as good.)

I have no shame bringing store-bought treats to a function, although I've learned there is one situation where it really isn't appropriate:

I once brought some pastries I had purchased at a local bakery to a church bake sale. Later that week, a friend and I were serving together in a ministry and she said something to me along the lines of "Someone actually brought store-bought items to Sunday's bake sale—*can you believe it!?*" (Yes. Yes, I could. Sigh.) Until then, I hadn't realized that the purpose of a bake sale was to sell things you had baked yourself—hence the word "bake."

90

Unconventional Ways to Serve Veggies

Sure, we would all love our kids to enthusiastically dive into a veggie stir-fry, complete with cauliflower and snow peas, but the reality is, many of us have a hard time getting greens into our little people. I have heard of children that eat bell peppers and radishes like apples, but, alas, that has not been my lot as a mom. Here are some ways I've found to make the job of feeding vegetables to our kids a little easier:

1) Layer fresh spinach in a lasagna, or sauté it and add it to an omelet. Steam it, squeeze out the excess water, mix it in mashed potatoes, and serve with cheese on top. You can also put it in sandwiches instead of lettuce. (This is super easy because spinach usually comes prewashed.)

2) You can add all sorts of sautéed vegetables (spinach, zucchini, mushrooms, onions, bell peppers) to a sweetened spaghetti sauce.

3) Boil finely diced carrots (or peas) with your macaroni noodles, and then mix it all together with the cheese sauce.

Elijah (3) said this to some peas that had fallen beneath the rim of his plate: "Quit hiding and get into my mouth!"

---

4) Cooked broccoli florets are good mixed in with cheesy, scrambled eggs. You can disguise the broccoli even further by wrapping it all up in a corn or flour tortilla.

5) Put out a plate of baby carrots and/or cherry tomatoes a half-hour or so before dinner to snack on. If kids are super hungry, they are more likely to eat them.

6) Take your kids grocery shopping and have them choose a vegetable that they have never tried before. Picking out something new themselves can make eating it more enjoyable.

7) Involve them in the preparation process. Snapping the ends off of green beans, washing lettuce, and shucking corn are great jobs for little hands. Good tasks for older kids are: shredding carrots, peeling potatoes, and slicing and sautéing zucchini. (I think one of the reasons some of my kids like zucchini so much is because I let them experiment with different seasonings when making it.)

8) Bacon makes Brussels sprouts much more appealing. Of course, pretty much anything with bacon is more appealing: bacon and green beans, bacon and spinach, bacon and asparagus, bacon in a green salad, *bacon with bacon* . . . (Just don't overdo it so that your kids start to think bacon is a vegetable.)

It is encouraging to remember that many children grow to become vegetable lovers (or at least lovers of *some* vegetables). It may have something to do with the fact that, as kids grow, their number of tastes buds diminishes, making strong-tasting foods more appealing. I was so surprised when both of my previously tomato-loathing boys decided, at separate times, that they wanted tomatoes on their In-N-Out burgers. And my daughter who once despised mustard, is now requesting it on her sandwiches. Having seen this with my older kids, I am much more relaxed with my younger children. (Our kids aren't the only ones who are growing!)

Again, life is more than food. (But then again, so much of life is about food—sometimes it can feel like, *Didn't I just feed you guys!?*) The Lord will be faithful to lead us as we feed our families. We can find peace resting in His leading, instead of obsessing over eating. We may even find ourselves making peace with food we never saw as a blessing before—I'm looking at you, ramen noodles!

Author and blogger Mary Ostyn created a great recipe with ramen noodles called "Jazzy Ramen Stirfry." You can find it on her website:

http://owlhaven.net/

One of my kids said, "It tastes just like the restaurant!"

CHAPTER 9

The Homemaking Balance

**When I was trying to convince Elijah (7), our
resident "packrat," to get rid of something on his
ridiculously cluttered desk, he protested, "No! . . .
Once in a while, I am so happy to have it!"**

There have been seasons in my life where I *really* needed to clean more. I recall being terribly embarrassed during one of these times when a friend stopped by midweek to get something, and the dirty dishes from the meal we had eaten with him *on Sunday* were still stacked up on the counter! Just lovely. I was new to being a homemaker and this laziness, which is what it was in my case, had carried over from my prodigal years. (When you have spent many years living to please yourself, creating a comfortable living environment for others is completely foreign territory.) During my early years of homemaking, the Lord used many Titus 2 teachings to instill in me a high view of this calling. It was more than just housework—it was a practical way to love Him and my family.

I love the acronym JOY. It stands for:

Jesus
Others
You

Put the People Before the Place

However, the pendulum swung too far (story of my life), and I found myself at the opposite end of the spectrum as a "neat freak." It has been my experience that neat freaks and little kids do not mix very well. Elijah (~3) once drew a picture of me vacuuming, with Esther (~2) standing right in front of the vacuum. It looked like I was just vacuuming her over. The Lord spoke to my spirit that, in essence, that is what I was doing with my fanatic cleaning. I had gone from a reluctant cleaner to a housemaid-on-steroids! And all the times I read about the importance of having a sparkling and tidy home only served to fuel my fanaticism—or reduce me to tears, when it wasn't possible for me to maintain with little ones underfoot.

My friend Robin wrote a blog post about all of the ways her toddler "helped" her in the house. It was just so helpful of him to take out her dish towels and kitchen utensils and scatter them across the floor so she could get to them more easily, and things like that. (The Lord used her sweet way of looking at things to teach me the importance of perspective.)

Walk by the Spirit, and You Will Not Gratify the Desires of the Flesh. -Galatians 5:16

Proverbs 14:1 says that the wise woman "builds her house," while the foolish one tears hers down with her own hands. I have done the latter, through both neglect of my house and over-focus on it. So, what is the balance? (To clarify, by "balance," I am *not* saying we are supposed to make everything equitable. What I am referring to is not letting something become such a focus that we neglect other things God has called us to.) I encourage you to ask the Lord how *He* wants you to care for your home, and then be sensitive to His

Spirit as you go about your day. If you are married, I also encourage you to ask your husband what he thinks about it. Knowing what is important to Mickey has been very helpful to me as I manage our home.

A great question to ask our husbands:

My friend Kay said, "I asked my husband if I could only get one extra thing done today, what would he like it to be."

How I wish I could speak as someone who doesn't get out of balance anymore! I can still find myself on both ends of the spectrum when it comes to housework, although I predominantly struggle with over-cleaning. While putting the "people before the place" is something I am still growing in, I can testify that the more I die to myself, the more God transforms me to see (as in, *really see*) things from His perspective. "Cleanliness is next to godliness" was said by Benjamin Franklin—it is *not* Scripture. We need to be careful not to elevate a clean house to a level that God never intended it to be. (To be clear, too much cleaning for one mom might be just right for another.)

Esther, looking in a picture Bible, pointed to an Old Testament character and said, "Here's Jesus!" Elijah corrected her, "No, Esther. Jesus wears a blue scarf and a white shirt." (How many things do we attribute to God that are really just man's depictions of Him?)

If the Lord is leading you to clean more, I encourage you to find joy in improving your home environment for the sake of others and His glory. You may also want to prayerfully reevaluate your time commitments. When things really start to unravel in my home and I know I need to be doing more, it is often an indication that I have overcommitted to one or more things. If you need to step it up in this area (or relax your cleaning efforts), the way to tackle the oftentimes seemingly insurmountable task is to *pray* and *obey*: pray for strength, and then obey in His power.

When Esther (~ 3) wanted to do something by herself she would say, "I want to do it—*by all myself.*" This is how we are in the flesh, sisters. We think we can do God's will "by all ourselves," but we can't. Without Jesus, we can do nothing (John 15:5).

Cleaning Tips

I have had to die, die, *and die again* to my desires for a level of clean that I'm just not able to enjoy in this season of my life, and have finally come to accept a lived-in look in my home (after all, we do live here, right?). Even so, I'm always open to new quick and easy cleaning techniques to help me keep my people clothed and my house in a functional state. Some of my corning-cutting tips are as follows:

Laundry

I actually don't mind folding laundry because I get to work while sitting down (perspective!), but when I haven't gotten around to it, we just sift through the piles to find something to wear. I also rarely fold washcloths, kitchen towels, and underwear. (I read about a mom who decided to simply stop folding her children's clothing altogether. They still hung up their nicer clothes, but everyday items were layered in drawers and plastic containers. You could even go simpler, like two sisters I know, and just give each child a large bin to toss their clean clothes into.)

I also do not match socks anymore during folding time. Instead, I just throw them into a hamper that stays tucked under my desk in the living room (another basket holds our matched socks). We make matches *occasionally*. When there aren't any pairs left, we can rummage through the basket and find a pair pretty easily. If not, wearing two different socks is something I have totally made peace with.

I hope to one day follow the rotation that I wrote into our routine, but cleaning bedding in my house is currently on a need-to-clean basis. I know that would be totally unacceptable to some people, but the nature of my busy life means I have had to let some things go. I honestly do not think my kids have been hurt by it at all—the only thing that has been hurt has been my pride. (Actually, some of my children frequently sleep out on our couches, or sometimes even on the floor, so their sheets stay cleaner longer anyway . . . which brings up a good point: where and when our children sleep is a Grey area.)

When I first met Mickey, I was surprised to learn he sorted his laundry by color. He literally had a rainbow of clothing piles scattered across his living room floor: red to purple with black and white. I tried his system for a while, but then, thankfully, realized such sorting isn't necessary. In fact, you really only need two categories: dark and light. So much easier than managing ten piles! The only thing I miss about that system is the pretty way it looked. *Sorry, honey . . .*

Great stain-prevention tips: Stay away from white clothing if you can! I try to keep us clothed mainly in prints and darker colors because they hide stains. And wearing aprons in the kitchen helps cut down on grease stains. If you do get grease on your clothes, apply Dawn dish soap (which is used to clean ducks that have been rescued from oil spill sites) to the spot and then throw it in the washer.

A great smell-prevention tip: If you ever forget to take your laundry out of the washer before it starts smelling like mildew, dump a cup or so of white vinegar over the load before you wash it again. It really helps to get the odor out.

Ironing Tip #1: This one I hardly ever follow, but if you take your clothes out of the dryer as soon as they are dry, they will not be nearly as wrinkled as they would be if you left them in there for a day or more. You can always also just throw a wet towel in with a load of wrinkled clothes and dry it for a while (it usually helps).

Ironing Tip #2: Buy wrinkle-free clothing whenever possible! Mickey frequently wears button-down shirts, and finding a brand that makes wrinkle-free ones has saved me so much time. (Even if you have to run an iron over them, it goes by much faster.) I also avoid purchasing any of those cotton sundresses for little girls that look so cute until their first washing, when they come out of the dryer wadded up into an unrecognizable ball of cloth.

Ironing Tip #3: Decide that wrinkles are a good "casual look" and just go with it.

Floors

Floor Tip #1: If you hate standing on crumbs, it is helpful to wear a pair of comfortable shoes in the house. Being an obsessive sweeper, I am less tempted to sweep when I shouldn't if I can't feel how dirty the floor is!

Floor Tip #2: Get a dog (they happily eat food scraps off the floor) … but then you have a whole new cleaning problem with the fur! We have been indoor-pet people for several years now, and I still have not gotten used to looking like a "Yeti" when I leave the house. Our dog and two cats have light colored fur, which really stands out on my wardrobe of black, grey, and darker grey. Sometimes, I wonder why it ever seemed like a good idea to invite animals to live inside a house that also houses seven children! We've also hosted polliwogs, dozens of ants (in an ant farm they tend to achieve pet status), caterpillars, an injured lizard, and, not even counting the peacock that hung out on our roof for the better part of a week, two wild birds. *Yes, wild birds.* One was a hummingbird with an injured foot; the other one just flew in for a visit one day and ended up building a nest in my girls' closet out of things like yarn, leaves from a silk plant, and, get this, a doll bib! You can't make this stuff up. But "Linda" and our cat didn't exactly get along, and let's just say the cat won . . .

---

*Looking at a veterinary coupon, Elijah (7) excitedly said, "Mom, guess what? These guys treat your pets *just like family!*"

*Eva (~6) said, "Esther's pet is the cat. Mine is Lizzie (the lizard we rescued). And Zeke's is the cocoon." (The lot of being child number four.)

Kitchen

I do not have a whole lot of corner-cutting tips for the kitchen because I enjoy washing dishes. In fact, when I am lost in thought about something, I often find myself scrubbing pots simply because it is my default setting. However, I have found some things to reduce our use of dishes, because a home of nine people produces a whole lot of kitchen work and my love for dish washing has its limits! One thing that has proved to be very helpful is that each of my kids has their own water cup on the kitchen counter. We have a bunch of them in four different colors that are easily turned into eight designated ones with rubber bands on half of them. (Hope that makes sense! I know what I'm talking about and still get confused when I read over that sentence.) Another great dishwashing-avoidance-method is to serve sandwiches and other finger foods on napkins instead of plates. Lastly, soaking saves so much time! And not just with pots and pans, but the stovetop, countertop, and fridge surfaces, as well. (It is important to note that you should wait until pots and pans cool down before you fill them with water—the drastic temperature change can cause them to warp.)

Microwave Cleaning Tip: Heat a cup of water in there for five to ten minutes (depending on how dirty it is), and then just wipe it clean. The steam does most of the work.

Bathrooms

I may enjoy folding laundry and washing dishes, but cleaning the bathroom is definitely *not* one of my favorite things to do. Therefore, I try to clean our bathrooms as fast as is humanly possible. I sometimes wipe down the counter and other surfaces while my little ones take a bath; when they splash outside of the tub, I just use a towel to "mop" the floor with the soapy water. And in my kid's bathroom, I don't use a bath mat anymore since it seemed to be in the washer more than on the floor. Now, I just throw a towel down, which is much easier to wash and dry.

When I am not in cleaning mode, but the toilet is in dire need of some help, I pour bleach into the bowl and just let it sit for a while before flushing. I use toilet paper to wipe down the outside so that I can flush it when I am done and do not have to wash anything. And, for when I am in cleaning mode, I love, love, *love* the disposable toilet wands, because the brushes tend to be toddler magnets like everything else gross you would never ever want them to touch or put in their mouths. (Didn't know parenting would be full of so many moments where I would be yelling "Gross! No!" and "*Whyyyyyyy?*" all at the same time!)

A Gross/No/Why moment:

Eva (1) was contentedly chewing on something. I fished it out of her mouth to find it was a soggy spider.

I used to get *so upset* when I would go into my kid's bathroom and see it in a state of disarray. Actually, "disarray" is too kind of a word—Indoor Monsoon Aftermath is a more accurate description.

Something physically awful would happen to me whenever I saw it like that. I still often flinch when I go to open the door. Some years ago, the Lord led me to ask myself two questions when I walk in on a mess: Is this something that I need to be training them in? Or is this one of those things that just takes time for them to get and I need to let it go? By asking those questions, rather than getting frustrated with the kids, I am encouraged to either give them grace or take responsibility to teach them something they need to learn or relearn. I praise God for His leading in this area because my incidents of panic attacks in the bathroom have significantly lessened.

Windows and Mirrors

Can you believe I used to equate sparkling windows with godliness? But my windows rarely sparkled, so they stood as continually smudged and streaked reminders that I just wasn't good enough. Praise God for freedom!

I do not clean the windows all that often, or I have my kids clean them, which sometimes looks worse *after* the cleaning, but at least they are marked with clean smudges, and I am seriously good with it! Some windows I only clean when company is coming over, and some I rarely clean (because who doesn't appreciate tinted windows in the bathroom?).

Expect the mess:

My friend Terry said that being a mom involves bringing order into our homes over and over *and over again*—messes are simply part of this calling. This perspective has helped me when I walk into an area that "I just cleaned!" or throw a load of towels into the washing machine that I am positive I just folded and put away yesterday *(if not ten minutes ago)*. If our focus is not on the seemingly endless repetition, but on loving our people and our King, the work can be transformed from a frustrating task into an act of love and worship.

Chore Time

Something very helpful that God has led our family in is that we do chores after every meal. Everyone, except for littles, is given an area to clean, which most often just keeps our home in what I have come to accept as a-manageable-state-of-varying-degrees-of-messiness (because our house is full of life and *life is messy!*). It helps me to let messes go throughout the day because I know we will get to them later. Before we had this in place, I was picking up all day long! I still pick up necessary items like those things that can't be left out for safety or stewardship reasons—I usually just toss them into various containers that I keep around the house for that very purpose. When they get full, I then put everything away.

Eva (11) was cleaning up the living room and my littles kept pulling toys out when she wasn't looking. Frustrated that they kept messing it up, she said, "I don't know how they do it—*it's their special power!*"

Cleaning Tip #1: When we don't have time to do a full chore, or things are just really messy, I sometimes call everyone and tell them to each pick up ten, twenty, or thirty things fast. (Just watch out for the kid that will find the loophole of picking up twenty crayons or thirty Cheerios off the carpet.)

Cleaning Tip #2: Let your kids pick out a favorite song and have them clean as fast as they can until it is done playing.

Cleaning Tip #3: Instead of giving time-outs, you can have your children pick up an area, clean out a vehicle, or, my new personal favorite, pick burrs out of clothing!

Cleaning Tip #4: You can also make cleaning a competition: give your little kids white socks to wear on their hands (this is a great use for socks that are missing their match), and tell them to dust around the house for five minutes or so to see whose sock can get the dirtiest.

Stuff Management

When it comes to toys, I like the motto "less-is-more"; although it often feels like we have "more-than-less." Still, I try hard to keep things to a minimum. If my kids do not play with something regularly, and I don't see a need for it in the foreseeable future, it usually gets donated. (Or thrown out, because no, packing peanuts are not a treasure!) Unfortunately, as my children have gotten older, they have occasionally purchased things that I *never* would have, and that I couldn't come up with a good reason to say no to. There are also times they have been gifted items that serve to only take up space in our small shed—like the old boat motor and bulky motorcycle bag my dad gave Elijah. We don't have a boat or a motorcycle, but usability isn't high on his list of reasons for keeping stuff. Since I am seriously allergic to clutter, this is truly an act of sacrificial love on my part. (Motherhood often requires more of us than we are capable of, but *God is able!*)

Eva (4) heard a motorcycle outside. She turned to me and said, "Mom, did you hear that furious sound?"

I used to go crazy, *and drive my family absolutely crazy,* looking for lost items. To avoid such unpleasantness, I came up with a great solution: I now have a whiteboard on the wall to list non-urgent lost items. There is a small monetary reward for each item found, which gives my kids the incentive to look for that lost shoe or whatever else happens to have been misplaced. Now, instead of running all over the house and turning all the couches inside out (and then having to fight the urge to scream because I just discovered five billion things under the cushions, but *not the one thing* I am presently looking for), I can simply write the item down, knowing that it will most likely be found—*eventually*. Preferably before they grow out of the missing shoe! But I have to confess that once the only three things on the whiteboard were:

Mom's black clog
Mom's black flip-flop
Mom's black sandal

I was obsessively looking for a pair of children's scissors. After having asked my kids for the 178th time where the blue scissors were, Elijah (~ 5) looked at me in exasperation and said, "We know about the blue scissors!" (Like, *"Enough already!"*)

Deep Cleaning

The word "deep" is subjective. My version of deep cleaning is probably considered basic cleaning to many others. On Saturdays (or any day after a Saturday or more have been missed), I try to have a cleaning morning when we do more detailed work in addition to our regular chores. Each of my older kids is assigned a room or two to clean, sometimes along with an outside chore. (I made lists for each room with all of the things needed to be done during both basic Chore Time and on Cleaning Day. I laminated them and then hung them on the walls of their respective rooms for easy reference.) Having a certain portion of time scheduled for this helps keep the toilet from turning into a black hole, the fridge from turning into a science experiment, and the floors from looking like we live in a barn because of all the straw tracked in from the backyard. (Laying down straw is a cheap substitute for a lawn—it is soft to play on, keeps the yard from getting muddy in the rain, and you don't have to water it!)

Children can be so random:

Eva (~ 5) left the room where she had been playing with the other kids, knelt on the ground, and pressed her nose to the floor for a couple of seconds. "Eva, what are you doing?" I asked. "Just smelling the carpet," she said matter-of-factly, and then traipsed on back to rejoin her siblings.

Lest you think this is some smooth-running operation, please know, it is still quite a challenge for me to get it all organized and overseen. (And by "challenge," I mean it sometimes feels like my own personal Mount Everest!) Part of this is due to the fact that I have no administrational abilities *whatsoever*—basically, my ducks are rarely in a row, and if they ever are, I am usually a wreck because of what it took to get them there! Another reason is that with kids training just takes time. Sure, one or two things may be relatively easy to train them in, but put together everything that we as parents need to teach our children (including all of the things you are surprised they have to learn—like, "butter is not a snack by itself"; "cart handles are not for chewing on"; and "the ceiling fan is *absolutely not* a merry-go-round!") and it is a monumental task. My friend Kay likens working with young children to how God allows us to work with Him: it may take more time and be messier, but it is how we learn!

A godly older woman in my life, Deborah Heberly, told me something in my early years of mothering that has often encouraged me to not lose heart and stay the course: "Raising children is a marathon—*not a sprint.*"

(If you do not have any Titus 2 sisters speaking wisdom into your life, I encourage you to prayerfully find some!)

Clean Car

Is it just me, or has anyone else ever thought that was sinful to have a dirty car? (Clearly, my legalism knew no bounds!) This was a problem for me because our vehicles are rarely clean in any shape or form. Not only is it *super* low on our list of things to do, but we don't have a garage, which means we have to park under trees laden with pollen, sap, and birds . . . *oh my!* We also live on a dirt road, and even though I have been known to make the rule that "we will never *ever* do it again as long as I live," we still eat in there at times, which can get super messy with seven children. I once vacuumed my Suburban and there was so much debris rattling around in the hose that it literally sounded like it was raining Skittles. I used to get *so embarrassed* when we would drive to church in our dust-covered van, but now, thanks to Mickey's insistence that it is not a sin issue, I can (mostly) pass by people in the church parking lot without feeling the overwhelming urge to slump down in my seat and avoid eye contact.

Arguments between siblings are never pleasant, but fights in the car seem to take it up a notch of misery for us mamas, don't they?

Zeke and Eva were fighting in the back seat of the car *over this*: "Eva said I have ten fingers, but I don't!"

We are instructed in Titus 2:5 to manage our homes, but this is not just for the sake of having a nice home in and of itself. Caring for our homes is ultimately for the purpose of serving our family and others for the glory of God. If keeping our house clean and organized starts hurting our family instead of helping them, we need to prayerfully re-evaluate our priorities. May the Lord lead you in the level of order and cleanliness that He has *for you*. It will look different for each of us. And remember, His burden is light!

My go-to cleaning "recipe" (for lack of a better word):

All-Purpose Cleaner

Fill a spray bottle half-full with white vinegar.
Fill the rest with water.

Add several drops of essential oil (lavender and lemon are my favorite) and a splash of vanilla (the kind you cook with).

*Shake well before using.

CHAPTER 10

Finding My Own Version of Beautiful

Zeke (3) cupped my face in his little hands one evening and tenderly said, "Mom, you look like a woman. You look like a *'bootiful'* woman."

My younger sister Lisa and I are opposite in a number of ways. As I shared in a previous chapter, I am obsessed with organizing and she is somewhat of a "stasher." We like to laugh about how she used to leave her home a wreck, yet look as if she had stepped off the page of a magazine (it is hit or miss now that she is a mom), while I (before a certain number of kids) could leave the house quite tidy but go out looking, umm . . . Let's just say that one day I passed by a mirror in Wal-Mart and was unpleasantly surprised to see a "rat's nest" sticking out on the back of my head! I even went shopping once with my maternity pants on backwards—the worst part of it was I had given my son a lecture earlier *that very day* about putting his clothes on the right way. I guess he comes by it honestly . . .

Instances like that abound in my life, and while I am trying to get better at it, I have slowly come to embrace my unique ministry— the ministry of messiness. Because no matter how hard I try, most Sunday mornings we tumble out of our vehicle looking somewhat rumpled and unmatched *(Why, oh why, do they put on that pair of shoes when you aren't looking???).* So, if the way my children and I look makes you feel better about the way your family looks, I am blessed to have been of service.

We may have some hair issues going on here:

*When Esther (5) saw my mom's "morning hair" for the first time, all she could come up with was an incredulous "*Why?*"

*I asked Eva (4) how I looked after she did my hair. She said, "Better than an elephant! Better than a giraffe! Better than a lion! Better than all of the animals at the zoo!" *(Definitely the look I was going for . . .)*

*Zeke (3) got his hair styled and said, "There aren't many hairs as nice as this hair!"

Be-YOU-tiful

Unlike me, my sister Lisa has a flair for what I would consider traditional beauty. She consistently produces professional looking photo books; I have thousands of pictures yet to develop. She sews ruffled aprons; I iron on patches. Her dinner parties are legendary; my dinner parties are extremely rare, *for a reason.* She makes cupcakes decorated in fancy designs like owl faces; I don't attempt cupcakes anymore because I cannot even ice them without tearing the tops! Her house is decorated like a display at Crate and Barrel; mine reflects more of a thrift store look. She makes sweats look like a designer outfit, while I make them look like, well, sweats. Actually, this is the case with both of my sisters. They got my dose of fashion sense (meaning I really have none at all), and when I have tried to copy the fashionable style of others, I usually just end up feeling like a fish out of water. But as I've matured in the Lord, I have grown to love our differences and accept my own, albeit unorthodox, version of beauty: In my younger years, it was interesting clothing combinations like culottes (remember those?) with tights underneath and tank tops over t-shirts. These days, I mainly wear things that are dark and comfortable. And if I find something that I absolutely love, I have no problem buying a bunch and wearing the same thing over and over *and over again*—it certainly solves the problem of not knowing what to wear!

Some clothing humor:

*I was sorting through some of the donations I was giving to our church's clothes closet. Elijah (7) held up one of my shirts and suggested I give it to a friend of mine who is a lot smaller than I am. I told him it would not fit her, but he insisted that she could "grow into it!" (I had to explain to him that adults do not generally try to grow into things.)

*I got "dressed up" (as in, not wearing pajama-type clothing and getting rid of my rat's nest—you know, *fancy*) one night to go to the grocery store. When I came out, Elijah (~8) exclaimed, "Mom, you look so nice—like you are going to visit King Agrippa!"

*Another time, at the age of seven, he was playing the groom in a wedding and asked me, quite seriously, "Do I look too shabby?"

Before I was freed to embrace my own unique style, I was burdened by something I had read by a Christian author. She had written that she always tried to make sure she was the best dressed at social events. This was not just a decision she had personally made, but one she was encouraging her readers to make, as well. I struggled with this teaching for quite some time, but the Lord graciously set me free to see that such a perspective totally misses His creativity. The day this dawned on me, I was at a women's conference and was looking around at the many sisters dressed oh, so differently (and probably wondering how I measured up), when the thought came to me that the varied appearances of God's daughters are, to a large extent, part of His design! Instead of judging myself and others, I was suddenly overwhelmingly thankful to Him for making us all so different.

Remember, the Bible says when we compare ourselves with one another we are without understanding (2 Corinthians 10:12). *Without understanding, sisters.* We really need to get this one. Whether we are condemning ourselves because we don't feel we measure up, coveting the looks, life, or living room of another woman, or looking down on others because they don't meet our personal style standards, we must remember that such comparisons are not of the Lord.

Creating at Home

If you are style-challenged like me, but still long to beautify your surroundings, take heart! There are a myriad of ways to create beauty in a home. Don't compare yourself with others. Instead, appreciate their gifts and enjoy the uniqueness of their homes. By all means, glean decorating ideas if you want, but you can also find your own unique ways of creating a beautiful living environment. Remember, "beauty is in the eye of the beholder." (It is also important to note that nowhere in the Bible is outward beauty commanded.) There is so much peace in embracing what we have been given and what we have been called to!

It used to drive me crazy how much my home and furnishings were falling apart, but God has really done an incredible work in my life in this regard. Now, many of the things that I used to find bothersome actually bring me joy, because they reflect my own personal version of "shabby chic" (as in, things are really starting to look shabby around here!), which I like to refer to as "Classic Kid." The more scratches, dents, and chips in my kitchen table, the more Classic Kid it looks. Not that we encourage our children to be poor stewards; we do want them to care for the things God has given us. But they are kids, and when your house is full of them, the Law of Entropy is accelerated!

The following examples are various ways I have found to bring my own version of beautiful into our home environment. Hope it serves as an encouragement that there are many ways to decorate a home:

- I love the following saying (cliché though it may be): "When life gives you lemons, make lemonade!" My toddler kept writing on the walls; we were not getting around to painting over it, so I decided to "make lemonade" by drawing a frame around one of the pictures and then signing her name. (There is a scene in the you-absolutely-must-see-it movie *Mom's Night Out*[22] where the main character hangs actual frames over her daughter's wall art.) Another time, one of my little ones drew multiple vertical lines on a wall. I took a Sharpie and turned those lines into stems by drawing leaves on them; I then drew flowers on top. To complete this work of art, I wrote Isaiah 40:8 underneath: "The grass withers, the flower fades, but the word of our God will stand forever."

Elijah (~4) told me that Jesus was wrapped in lemons while He was in the tomb. I corrected him by saying, "I think you mean linens." He said, "Yah—*lemons!*"

- They probably got the idea to write on the wall from me. Desperate to be surrounded by the Word, I grabbed a Sharpie one day and started writing Scripture all over my house—many of our walls ended up with verses on them, along with a lot of door trim and even the oven hood! This is a decorating idea I took directly from the Old Testament: in Deuteronomy 11:18–20, God commanded the Israelites to

---

[22] Drew, Sarah, Sean Astin, Patricia Heaton, David Hunt, Andrea Logan White, and Trace Adkins. *Mom's Night Out*. DVD. Directed by The Erwin Brothers. Los Angeles: TriStar Pictures, 2014.

lay up His words in their hearts and souls, and "write them on the doorposts" of their houses and gates.

- I have decided to view the ever-changing mountain of laundry on our "folding couch" as a living piece of modern art. It is always changing—who knows what it will look like next! (And it has the added benefit of being a very comfortable backrest when I sit down to watch movies. Perspective, right?)

- We tested those shatter-resistant Corelle dishes for several years and our findings were conclusive—if they fall at a certain angle (and with children they tend to fall frequently), you can expect them to explode into a gazillion little pieces. Tired of sweeping up shards of glass, I made the switch to plastic. (Sorry, Corelle. Your patterns really are quite lovely.) Wal-Mart sells a brand of bowls and dishes (called Nordicware) that is inexpensive and dishwasher- and microwave-safe. The magic three!

- The doorframe on our bathroom shower stall was stained with mold and impossible to clean, so I took a hammer to it one day and just ripped it out. Then, I chipped off the adhesive and purchased bathtub appliques to go over the holes where the hardware had been. I put up a shower curtain and ended up with a super cheap bathroom remodel!

- The little window in our bathroom got an arc-shaped crack, so I took some oil pastels and colored in a rainbow over it.

- I decided to involve everyone in the decorating by hanging my children's artwork from clothespins attached to strings that are stretched across the tops of our walls. (My mom puts up her grandkids' pictures with toothpaste! Just put a little on each corner of the paper, press it on the wall, and it stays put.)

*Zeke (3) drew a "picture" on my dad's Father's Day card. I asked him what it was, expecting him to say "dog" or "truck" or something like kids usually do. Instead, he said, matter-of-factly, "It's a scribble!" (*Obviously . . .*)

*Eden (~5) was showing something to her brother that one of the kids had created. "Look Zekie! Isn't it awesome? Isn't it amazing?" Zeke (~7) had a different opinion: "No . . . *it's dramatic.*"

- I like to put peel-and-stick whiteboard and chalkboard sheets over damaged places on walls and cupboards (of which we have many). I have them all over my house with Bible verses, notes, and even recipes (in the kitchen) written on them. They are also great for putting on bathroom doors with the *oh, so necessary* reminder to "Please KNOCK!"

- I really wanted to surround my kids with pictures of God's creation. Instead of purchasing framed pictures, I decided to just display various coffee-table books (over-sized picture books that are frequently found at thrift stores). You can buy book holders for this purpose, or just prop them up on a shelf with a small item in the middle to keep the pages open.

- Before we bought individual lockers for our kids, we turned the wall by our front door into a "coat wall" by hanging up a bunch of hooks. It really worked with my Classic Kid look, and brought a lot of color into our living room.

- One of my sons (yes, the infamous Zeke, who is actually now one of our most mild- mannered children . . . *go figure)* decided to poke a ton of holes in our bathroom and bedroom walls. Naturally, we thought we had termites, because who would have ever thought that someone would think poking sheetrock with a screwdriver a hundred times was the definition of a good time. I digress . . . So, Elijah (12) was given the task, by my husband mind you, to install termite poison . . . unsupervised . . . with a power tool . . . (ahem). He proceeded to drill about a dozen large holes along the baseboard of my bathroom wall. *Oye ve!* What's a mom to do? I took spackle and smeared it over the holes in a textured, grass-like design, and made a big heart over the pseudo-termite holes. I also did this in my kid's bathroom: I spackled more grass-like shapes over gouges and scrapes on the walls, while one of my girls made designs shaped like bees. After it dried, we took the same paint the rest of the bathroom had been painted with and just brushed it over our artwork. It looks like creative texturing that I like to think of as "Practical Art."

When my kids make foolish decisions, I should try to remember the following:

As a teenager, I once dyed my hair and got a large dye stain on the living room carpet. My parents weren't home for me to explain what had happened, and I had to go somewhere, so I put a box over it with a note that said something along the lines of "Don't Move!" (The worst part is, I'm pretty sure I expected them to leave it there!)

- I don't scrapbook. I think it is a really nice way to preserve memories, but it just isn't something I have ever felt led to do. I don't even put together photo albums anymore, so I hung up some of those cloth covered boards with the ribbons stretched across them to tuck photos into. It is such an easy and inexpensive way to display our pictures.

With my first two children, I had individual photo albums with the Biblical meaning of their names written on the front. Inside, the albums were full of baby pictures.

My third child, bless her heart, had a similar album, but it was far less filled.

My fourth child, *may he forgive me,* had his own album, but it remained empty because I never developed his baby pictures. Still haven't.

The same is true of my three youngest children.

Thankfully, I can now put our pictures on my computer as a rolling screen saver or plug them into a digital photo frame. Gone are the days of life on the prairie when you were lucky to get one black-and-white photograph of your family, looking rather stoic and slightly uncomfortable. (Although, come to think of it, that is how I look in most pictures . . .) I can either bury myself in guilt because I am not up on my photos, or I can thank God that we have photographs in the first place! *I'll go with thankfulness.* In the words of a sweet little vegetable (Veggie Tales):

"A thankful heart is a happy heart!"[23]

- When one of my boy's dresser drawers broke, I stripped all of the hardware out of the place where the drawer had been and turned it into a shelf to store clothes. Broken drawers that are otherwise still useful, can be placed on top of a dresser to store clothing, or repurposed to store other items around the house. I have one on the counter where I keep miscellaneous things, and, since scissors tend to go the way of lost socks in our home, I tied shoelaces to

---

[23] *Madame Blueberry.* DVD. Directed by Mike Nawrocki. Franklin: Big Idea Entertainment, 2012.

the knobs and then tied scissors to the laces so that we have them around whenever we need them. (This also works great with hairbrushes!)

- One of my kitchen cupboard doors came off and I realized I actually prefer having the cupboard open, because it makes accessing my bowls and other cookware easier. Plus, I can sit on a chair and use the bottom shelf as a footrest. (Looking for the good in things truly works wonders.)

Christmas traditions can be simple, yet meaningful:

My friend Kay set up a nativity scene, but the manger didn't have baby Jesus in it. Next to the scene was a basket of gold tinsel. Whenever someone performed a random act of kindness, without broadcasting it to everyone, he or she would place a piece of tinsel into the manger to get it ready for baby Jesus. He then showed up in the manger on Christmas Day. *Love this!*

- For Christmas, I place my children's socks "by the chimney with care." I do love the look of festive, monogrammed stockings, but nothing warms my heart like the sight of the eclectic sock assortment gathered around our stove.

While teaching about the three wise men to my Sunday School class, I got to the part about the gifts they brought to Jesus: "gold, frankincense, and myrrh." Charlie (4) quickly added, "...and hot chocolate!"

- I once purchased two large bushes to decorate as "Christmas trees." The idea was to enjoy them all covered in lights during December, and then put them in my front yard at the start of the new year.

Esther (3) bit a Christmas light bulb and, according to Elijah (4), "swallowed it *all the way down to her brain!*"

- I really wanted a long bench against the front of our house, so Mickey took some bricks that were just lying around our yard and made two pillars. He then laid a wide piece of old wood across them. Instant bench! (It just needs a sign that says, "Please sit down gingerly, and don't wiggle around too much.")

- The deer kept eating every colorful thing I planted. *Every single one.* I finally decided to stop wasting money and go with what deer will not eat: basically, lavender, rosemary, a little more lavender, and a lot more rosemary!

Think how boring it would be if our homes all reflected the same style and expressions of creativity. What is the point of having a patchwork quilt if all the squares are the same? One of the reasons we enjoy visiting one another's homes is because they are different. There is such peace in being content with who we have been created to be and with what we have been given to create with: "*Godliness with contentment is great gain, for we brought nothing into the world, and we cannot take anything out of the world*" (1 Timothy 6:6, 7—emphasis mine).

Headed Home

May we never forget that a believer's true home is in heaven. Having such an eternal perspective will keep our eyes focused on *all* that we have in Christ—and will have in the ages to come! Let's just let these promises about our forever home wash over us for a moment:

Here we have no lasting city,
but we seek the city that is to come.
-Hebrews 13:14

"In my Father's house are many rooms.
If it were not so, would I have told you
that I go to prepare a place for you?
And if I go and prepare a place for you,
I will come again and will take you to myself,
that where I am you may be also."
-John 14:2, 3

As it is written, "What no eye has seen,
nor ear heard, nor the heart of man imagined,
what God has prepared for those who love him."
-1 Corinthians 2:9

The following quote is from the rhyming children's book *The Bridge from OneDayBow*, which was written by my friend Kathy Warden. It is a wonderful story about the need for believers to walk through this life (represented by a town called "HereAndNow") suited in the armor of God, as we look forward to a glorious eternity in His Presence:

Be on guard and alert! Though you do not know the day,
The Son will come to get you and take you all away,
What has been prepared for you is beyond anything
That you can see, hear, or think—you'll live there with the King![24]

Jesus is preparing a place for us *where He resides*, sisters! I cannot even imagine the splendor that awaits us. Creation is a giant piece of spectacular artwork; our God is a Master Decorator—no one does beautiful like Him!

---

[24] Warden, Kathy. *The Bridge from OneDayBow*. Bloomington: WestBowPress, 2016. 128.

Elijah (3) and Esther (2) watched a children's movie with an animated chicken. Something about that chicken absolutely terrified them, and for *many* months after, we prayed at night for God to protect them from "the chickens and the monsters." One morning, Elijah told me that God had come into his room that night, taken the chickens away, and said, "I will save you." Then he told me that Jesus put a ladder behind our house and took them up to heaven. "What did you do in heaven?" I asked. "Saw Jesus," he said matter-of-factly. I asked him what heaven looked like and he exclaimed, "Light! We walked with Jesus too." He then said there were "lots of walking people" and that Jesus "made the people better." I'm not sure what happened that night, but what I do know is that God took care of those chickens!

CHAPTER II

Navigating the Sea of Choices

**Elijah, commenting on "marbled" playdough
(that short window of time before
mixed playdough turns an unknown color),
said, "This is so beautiful, Mom!
With the red and the green, it looks just like the ocean . . ."
I was totally with him until he added,
"... after a shark attack!"**

I believe the Lord uses the whole "birth plan" thing to introduce us to the fact that having and raising children is unpredictable. I had the *perfect* birth plan with my first pregnancy:

> Massage Lotion: check
> Soothing Music: check
> List of things I did not EVER want to happen (Number One item on that list—*No C-section!*): check

God's birth plan for me was somewhat different: I never cracked open the lotion or heard one musical note. I also ended up having a C-section. Seven C-sections later, I just have to laugh and am reminded of the following verse: "The heart of man plans his way, but the LORD establishes his steps" (Proverbs 16:9).

*When Eva (~6) was dictating a letter for her pen pal, she said, "I want to say that my mom popped out six kids."

*Another time, as if I was some kind of a baby vending machine, she requested that I have "eightlets."

My Times Are in Your Hand
-Psalm 31:15

Just as each one of my children's births was planned by God, every one of our days were written before one of them even came to be (Psalm 136:16), and God has prepared good works for believers to walk in throughout those days (Ephesians 2:10). Mamas, we can trust that as our believing children seek to be led by the Lord, He will direct their paths, open and close doors, and provide all that they need to walk in the things He has *already planned* for them. I cannot even begin to express the peace that has come as I rest in this. Of course, I am fully aware that my children have free will, and the cry of my heart is that they would choose to surrender all aspects of their lives to Him. It is a mystery, but even as you intercede out of deep concern for your loved ones in prayer, you can experience the peace that comes from trusting in the Lord.

All of my children's names start with the same letter, which gets trickier the more kids you have! When I was pregnant with baby number six, some of my older kids came up with the name "E-Bob."

(After much deliberation, we decided to go with the more traditional "Elizabeth," although we have called her "Lulu" for so long that when I once asked Mickey how to spell her real name, he had to ask me *what it was*! True story.)

Knowing the Lord is sovereign (which can be defined as being "in control") is a life preserver in the sea of life's choices. Choices are great, but, in the midst of them, we must never forget that "the way of man is not in himself, that it is not in man who walks to direct his steps" (Jeremiah 10:23). As we follow our Shepherd, we will be led in the unique paths He has carved out for our families. What peace there is in resting in the knowledge that, from the big decisions to the smaller ones, God will lead. This truth has transformed the way I view all of the options available to us as parents.

Since Mickey and I are called to homeschool our kids (and by no means am I saying this is *the way* to educate your children), there are many educational methods and materials for us to choose from. I used to get absolutely overwhelmed by the glossy catalog pages and persuasive articles on different educational approaches and philosophies. And what about extras like music lessons, sports, and art? Was I keeping Eva from realizing her calling to be a world-class painter because she wasn't getting professional instruction? Would Ezekiel miss being drafted into the NBA because we didn't get him onto the courts by the age of seven? Would Elijah never realize his full potential as a classical guitarist because we could barely get the basics done, let alone music lessons? Was Esther missing out on becoming a French chef because the only cooking instruction she was getting was from someone who cannot even ice a cupcake? *Have mercy!*

The answer to all of these questions is "No." When we are walking in God's will, seeking to be led by Him in the details of our lives, our children will not miss out on any opportunity He has for them. And even when we make mistakes and take wrong turns, our God is bigger than that! If His plan is for one of my children to be a "jungle doctor" (Zeke's future profession of choice when he was little), then I fully believe He can make that happen, and I do not have to sit around wringing my hands because we aren't using the best science curriculum available.

Mommy Brain strikes again:

Once "someone I know" (a friend of a friend's third cousin twice removed) totally spaced it and told her children that the fuzzy caterpillar they had found would turn into a bumblebee . . . (Thankfully, one of them knew his stuff and was able to correct this.)

For those of you who have been led to put your kids in school, the question of *where* can be just as daunting. My friend Kay said, "In fifth grade, my son wanted to be homeschooled. I was willing, because I could see junior high approaching. Where he was supposed to go to junior high was not a good fit for his personality. (At this large school, even the teachers did not have their own rooms; everything was fluctuating. My son needed structure and a close connection with his instructors.) However, my husband was of a different mind. He requested I look into all other options. Eventually, my son transferred to a different, but small, public school." This is a good example of how the Lord leads us in what is His best for our unique families and individual children.

There was a year my kids went to school. At the start of the school year, Elijah (~5) tried to convince me that we should let him stay home so he could "grow the crops." *(Nice try, buddy . . .)*

Having our kids go to a school was a great experience for me, because having had my kids both at home for school and out of the house for school has shown me that they each have their share of challenges. When you are tempted to compare what you have to do with what God has called someone else to, remember that every plot of grass has its own set of weeds to pull!

In his book *LIES Homeschooling Moms Believe*, Todd Wilson writes to moms:

> You can skip zoology altogether, and if your son was created to be a zoologist, he will become a zoologist. I've heard countless stories of how a mother was shocked by what her son or daughter became because she never taught them anything about those areas.
>
> Some have become computer "geeks" even though there were no computers in their house growing up. Some have become builders, taxidermists, engineers, lawyers, and doctors in spite of what they were or weren't taught from home.
>
> *They became what they became because that's what God created them to be.*[25] (emphasis mine)

Children can be taught from an early age that God is the Master of their lives:

Eva (5) said when she grows up, *"if God says yes,"* she will have: "One hundred turkeys . . . no, two. *[This seemed like a prudent decision.]* Two horses; two cows; two pigs; two chickens; two fire doggies; and two skunks." (She said this before she was sprayed in the face by a skunk—I'm sure her list looks a little different now!)

While I know that God's plans for my children are not dependent upon me, I also do not want to miss any part He has for me to play in shaping their lives (although I have missed a great many, am

---

[25] Wilson, Todd. *LIES Homeschooling Moms Believe*. Milford: Familyman Ministries, 2006. 90.

sure to miss more, and need much grace). Trusting in God does not mean taking a lackadaisical "oh, it will all work out" attitude. Absolutely, He is in control, but we must also take our roles and responsibilities seriously! Would any of us forgo using car seats? We trust that God is sovereign over life and death, but, at the same time, know He uses us to protect our children from harm. I don't know how it all works together, but what I do know is that our part matters *(car seats, right?)*.

It is a profound mystery—our part and His. I believe the key is found in not trying to figure it all out, but, as the hymn says, in choosing to simply "trust and obey, for there's no other way to be happy in Jesus, but to trust and obey"! So, my fellow mamas, let us trust the Lord with our children, as we wholeheartedly embrace this amazing calling we have been given to influence them for time and eternity.

Faithful = Successful

George Washington Carver (inventor of peanut butter; therefore, hero to many mothers) said, "The secret to my success? It is simple. It is found in the Bible: 'In all thy ways acknowledge Him and He shall direct thy paths.'" Most people will not achieve success in the way Mr. Carver did, but when we walk in the paths God has set before us, we will be successful by having done well as good and faithful servants of the King! Many of the things written about education have as their goal the making of children into "successful" adults. As Christian parents, we need to remember that success in God's economy is measured by faithfulness—being good and faithful servants (Matthew 25:23). What is most important to me regarding my children's education is that it prepares them for whatever God has called them to as His servants:

Only one life, 'twill soon be past,
Only what's done for Christ will last.[26]

---

[26] Studd, C.T. "Only One Life 'Twill Soon Be Past."

A great book for your teens to read is *Kisses from Katie: A Story of Relentless Love and Redemption*[27]:

It is the true story of an American teenager who was called to be a missionary (and adoptive mother to thirteen girls!) in Uganda.

When I walked away from the Lord as a teenager, "freedom" and "finding myself" was my mantra. How foolish and deceived I was, for "'whoever finds his life will lose it, and whoever loses his life for [Jesus'] sake will find it'" (Matthew 10:39). This word "find" means "to gain, procure, obtain,"[28] while the word "lose" is defined as "wholly destroyed."[29]

I left looking for freedom, but found myself enslaved to my flesh and the world instead. Into my late thirties, I am still learning the lesson that Katie grasped at an early age and is living fully—true freedom is found in dependence upon and service to the King. A note in the ESV Study Bible (for James 2:12) says, "True freedom is freedom to obey God and do what pleases him."[30] We were created for this, sisters! So were our kids. Let's make sure we teach them these truths. May they embrace death to self that they might live abundant lives in Christ!

I may end up raising the next Billy Graham or Kay Arthur. I may also raise children who are called to be custodians and scrub toilets for the glory of God, or missionaries who work in obscurity. Whatever they are called to do, if they are faithful, they will have

---

[27] Davis, Katie. *Kisses from Katie: A Story of Relentless Love and Redemption.* Brentwood: Howard Books, 2012.

[28] Spiros, Zodhites Th.D. *The Complete Word Study Dictionary: New Testament.* Chattanooga: AMG Publishers, 1992. 681-682.

[29] Ibid., 230-231.

[30] Taken from the ESV® Study Bible (The Holy Bible, English Standard Version®), copyright © 2008 by Crossway, a publishing ministry of Good News Publishers. Used by permission. All rights reserved.

been supremely successful in this life! In all honestly, I still battle against worldly desires for my kids, but God has done such a work in me that the overarching desire of my heart is for them to walk in the good works He has written for them and, in doing so, glorify Him with their lives. May we never forget that faithfulness equals success in God's economy. And may we find peace knowing that we can trust God to lead us as we seek to help our children find success *His* way.

---

*Elijah (11) said, "Whenever we start a new section in math, it is really easy." "That is because they are doing review," I told him. In all seriousness, he argued, "No, they just want to make us feel welcome."

*Lulu (6) was practicing her letter sounds. Looking at a page of pictures that started with the letter "G," she got to the gorilla and said, "Ga-ga-ga-ga-*gamonkey!*"

Life Is Learning

Something else I used to get really down about was preschool, because I had made a law in my mind that if I were going to be a godly mother I just *had* to teach preschool. I used to have a very nice set of educational toys for preschool-aged children, and while my little ones enjoyed playing with them, I had a hard time making teaching with those items a regular part of our day. This was often a source of guilt for me, as if I was depriving them, yet so much of life is learning! They can learn colors by playing a specific color-sorting game *or* by helping you sort laundry. They can learn to say their numbers by counting pegs *or* by counting to ten before they jump off of something. And they can easily learn to recognize their numbers by playing Go Fish or UNO.

Playing UNO, Zeke got a card that he did not like. I thought it was so funny when I heard him mutter: "Revolting!" (He got it from the book *Gregory the Terrible Eater.*[31])

And don't underestimate the power of a good DVD! I am a firm believer that quality movies, like the 1989 classic *Milo and Otis*,[32] are a good form of education. (You can learn a lot from that movie, you know. Like, cats definitely do not like water, dogs are quite loyal, deer like to frolic, and other highly scientific observations that escape me at the moment . . .) Put on an actual nature show and it is basically a science book on the screen! (I am just going to ignore the fact that Mickey is most likely rolling his eyes if he is reading this—unfortunately, he doesn't share my appreciation for the art of film.) There is also the added benefit of the break it provides from the noise and movement of one's children!

*"Motis and Lo" is what Eva used to call the movie *Milo and Otis*. Still puts a smile on my face!

*After Zeke watched *Old Yeller*,[33] he liked to talk about how "Old Gellar got the 'grabies.'"

Something we *do need to do* with our littles is make sure we are giving them the attention and affection they need. One of my younger girls told me she knew I loved her, but that she didn't think I liked to

---

[31] Sharmat, Mitchell and Jose Aruego. *Gregory, the Terrible Eater.* New York: Scholastic Paperbacks, 2009.

[32] *The Adventures of Milo and Otis.* DVD. Directed by Masanori Hata. Culver City: Columbia Pictures, 1998.

[33] McGuire, Dorothy, Fess Parker and Chuck Connors. *Old Yeller.* DVD. Directed by Robert Stevenson. Burbank: Walt Disney Pictures, 1957.

spend time with her. *Ouch.* I sadly realized I had been communicating that by saying no too much when she asked to play games with me. Sure, sometimes I couldn't, but there were other times I had wrongly prioritized lesser things over my relationship with her. And this may be just a brief season of her wanting to spend her free time with me! It really does go by fast, sisters.

I need to learn to pay attention better:

*Elijah (~5) was telling me something, but I was preoccupied and wasn't giving him my full attention. I mumbled, "Mmm-hmm, I see. I see." "No, you can't see when you are looking down!" he protested. (Kids really have a way of calling it like they see it, don't they?)

*Once, Eden (7) told me that Lulu wouldn't share the toilet (meaning she had been on it too long). Distracted, I gave my standard answer when they are fighting over something: "Can you share it?" (*The toilet!?* They thought this was hilarious!)

*Another time, Eden complained that Lulu had taken the toilet from her. It was obvious that I wasn't really listening because I told her to bring it to me. (When they argue over stuff, we often take the item away for a while—but the toilet is certainly an exception!)

In this day and age, we are bombarded with ideas, many of which have to do with educating our children. For those of you with little ones, don't forget that God provides so many natural learning opportunities for them throughout the day. If you are on idea overload, here's a suggestion: Go outside and just let them play in the dirt, inspect spider webs, and watch ladybugs. Fill the sink with water and tear-free soap, and let them play with some plastic dishes. Put on a worship CD and dance. A relaxed mom is better than designer macaroni art and edible play dough, right?

Mickey came home from work and Elijah (4) asked him, "How was your day?" He said it had been good. Then Elijah asked, "*Did you do any crafts?*"

Whether you are training toddlers or taming teenagers, as you teach, let God lead. Hear again His heart for us mamas: He will "gently lead those that are with young" (Isaiah 40:11). We can trust Him to teach us how to train up our children in the way that they should go (Proverbs 22:6). We can hope and pray that they will respond to the Gospel, and find comfort in knowing it is also God's desire for them to be saved (2 Peter 3:9). And in the midst of an intelligence-glorifying, achievement-driven, and materially-focused culture, we can ask the Lord to keep our hearts focused on what truly matters and to help us teach our children to do the same:

Thus says the Lord:
"Let not the wise man boast in his wisdom,
let not the mighty man boast in his might,
let not the rich man boast in his riches,
but let him who boasts boast in this,
that he understands and knows me,
that I am the LORD who practices steadfast love,
justice, and righteousness in the earth."
–Jeremiah 9:23, 24

Elijah (6) was telling Esther he knew something about the Bible that she didn't. When I corrected him for bragging, he said (referring to Jeremiah 9:23 and 24), "But God says we are to boast about Him!"

CHAPTER 12
"Matchmaker, Matchmaker, Make Me a Match"[34]

Eden (7) told me that when she gets married, she does *not* want to kiss—she would like to "stomp on bottles instead." At first, I didn't know where that came from, but then remembered the wedding scene from Fiddler on the Roof[35] where they do something similar.

In a book about battling legalism for mothers, I couldn't overlook this topic: marriage and the process leading up to it. My children may not be at the marrying age yet, but Mickey led a young adult group for a decade, which gave us significant exposure to this issue. And as much as I have learned about it, I know that nothing can truly prepare me for the bittersweet process of watching my children leave our family to start their own. I am pretty sure I will be ugly crying my way through the mother-son dance—*I've already cried just thinking about it!*

---

[34] Bock, Jerry and Sheldon Harnick. *Fiddler on the Roof*. DVD. Directed by Norman Jewison. Beverly Hills: Metro Goldwyn Mayer Studios, Inc., 1971.
[35] Topol, Norma Crain, Leonard Fray, Molly Picon, and Paul Mann. *Fiddler on the Roof*. DVD. Directed by Norman Jewison. Beverly Hills: Metro Goldwyn Mayer Studios, Inc., 1971.

*When he was ten, Elijah told me he planned on taking his prospective wife shopping to see how full her cart got before he decided to marry her. (Apparently, serious life decisions like marriage can be decided in the aisles of Wal-Mart!)

*He also thought it would be a good idea to keep wedding costs down by picking out the bride's dress *himself*. (Good luck with that one, buddy.)

Fiddler on the Roof is one of my favorite movies, and I especially love the song "Matchmaker" where Tevya's three daughters sing about their desires for a "perfect match," while still acknowledging that they are at the mercies of the local matchmaker. Matchmaking, in this sense, may be a practice foreign to our western culture, but the desire for a perfect match is not. This desire is shared by parents, as well. How we long for our children to choose the right spouse! Therefore, it is no surprise that many in the church have strong opinions regarding the process leading up to marriage. I mean, we are talking about our kids leaving us to cleave to another, so I totally get the level of concern.

---

*One day, on the playground, a little girl told my nephew Aaron (4) that she loved him. He just responded by yelling, "Barbeque Sauce!"

*Eva (4) said, "I'm gonna' tell you who I'm going to marry." She leaned over to whisper in my ear and said, "Don't tell anybody." Then she stood back and shouted out his name.

However, these opinions can easily turn into legalism, as has been the case in recent decades. It seemed that more and more detailed instructions were emerging as to the "right way" to date, court, or become engaged. It was confusing, to say the least. But there isn't one right way to get to know the person you hope to marry. Certainly, couples considering marriage who are still under the authority of their parents should obey them, and those who are adults should seek to honor ("weigh heavily"[36]) their parent's counsel. And yes, they should walk in love, be pure, live above reproach, and be guided by the Spirit. But a couple can do all of the above and still get to know one another in very different, yet God-honoring, ways.

---

*Elijah's kindergarten teacher was teaching them about the Ten Commandments and he said he knew one (the 8th): "A man with a woman can't take another man's woman."

*Eva (~5) asked me a question about marriage and started out by saying, "Mommy, *if your man* . . ."

"I Will Make Him a Helper Fit for Him."
-Genesis 2:18

There was also the idea of "The List." Maybe you have heard of it (or had one of your own). It is the one young singles are sometimes encouraged to write, listing all the things they want in a spouse. They should all be looking for fruit pertaining to salvation, of course, because, sadly, there are those who profess Christ but do not have true saving faith. But these lists tend to go beyond that, and have the potential to get pretty long. Please do not get me wrong! Lists are fine, but they *must be subject to the Lord.* For example, your daughter may want to marry a man without debt. *You* may want your daughter to marry a man without debt. Then, in waltzes "the one"—with a huge student loan. But if he is God's Mr.

---

[36] Baker, Warren, D.R.E. and Eugene Carpenter, Ph.D. *The Complete Word Study Dictionary: Old Testament.* Chattanooga: AMG Publishers, 2003. 491.

Right for her, she needs to trust Him and cross that requirement off her list. *You too.* We need to make sure we are letting God write our children's stories.

Not long ago, I fell into the trap of planning one of my children's futures: Mickey and I had been at a church retreat where, during a time of corporate prayer, an older missionary shared that he felt called to come alongside and disciple the new generation of missionaries in our church body. I felt my daughter Esther impressed upon my heart, and interpreted that to mean she was called to follow in his footsteps into Thailand (the country in which he had been ministering for a number of years). She had felt called to mission work for some time, and the Lord had also put a special love for Thailand on my heart, so it just seemed right that He would be calling her there. After that prayer meeting, I discovered a missionary card at our church with a picture of a missionary family from Thailand. Well, wouldn't you know, they have a son who looked to be a couple years older than Esther. *It was clearly a perfect match!* I was almost certain this was the young man God had chosen for her to marry after she (most likely) moved to Thailand as a missionary. I put the card up on our fridge, and yes, pointed him out to her a number of times. I tried to do so subtly, but she immediately knew what I was doing. Around this time, I also heard there might be an upcoming short-term mission trip to Thailand. *Of course* Esther should go, I reasoned. Not only could she visit the place she was (probably) soon moving to, but she would even get a chance to meet her (possible) future husband! (I gave allowances for the fact that I really didn't know for certain, but let's be honest—*I was pretty sure!*)

When I was told a trip was indeed taking place, I was so excited! I planned. I prayed. I even inadvertently pressured her to go with stories about how wonderful and life-changing the trip would be. At first, she seemed interested in going, but as time went on, her interest waned. And then, she came to me with the news that sent my hopeful plan for her beautiful future crumbling to the ground— she didn't feel called to go on the trip, and though she wasn't ruling it out that God could call her there someday, she was definitely not feeling called there at all presently. But I had been so close to sure! And then I realized that was the problem—I was sure of something apart from God's leading. While I do believe the Lord put her on my heart that night regarding some kind of mission work, I took it way beyond that and gave a place (and even a person for her to marry) to that calling. And I didn't even realize the extent of what I had done until the Lord revealed to me my error of going before Him . . . *way before* Him. Through that very humbling experience, I was reminded that I need to let God plan my children's futures.

Cake—quite possibly the single most inspirational word in the English language:

*Esther was preparing one of her younger siblings for a wedding. She told them, "You'll have to sit still, *but there will be cake!*"

*My mom texted me to see what our Sugar Lu (yes, that is her actual nickname) wanted for her birthday dinner. I jokingly texted, "Cake." "That is what Dad said she would say," she texted back. I then asked Lu what she wanted for her birthday dinner. In true Sugar Lu fashion, she said, "You mean my cake?"

Single-minded

In the midst of a church culture that esteems marriage so highly (and rightly so), it is important to know that our children may be called *not* to marry. We must remember that the call to singleness is also a high and holy calling. Single Christians are free to serve the Lord in ways their married counterparts are often unable to (1 Corinthians 7:32–34). I just spoke with an unmarried woman who is going on two international mission trips, back-to-back. I am happy to be married, but can still appreciate the blessing of being able to serve the Lord in such a way. Singlehood is a gift, just as marriage is. We need to teach this to our children so that they do not think they are "less than" in their single years, whether those years last for a brief time or for the remainder of their lives.

Jesus Is Enough

A number of years ago, I received a letter from a young woman in our church, asking my advice regarding what things I thought potential spouses needed to agree upon before entering into marriage. The following is based on my response to her:

Hi sister,

First, I want to say that I can only imagine what a difficult place it could be as a young woman in today's culture desiring a godly man to marry. And then, you have the added confusion of all the opinions in the Christian community regarding how to go about the marriage process in a God-honoring way. I say I can only imagine because I was not mature in the Lord when I got married, and was certainly unaware of *all* the ways people thought we should go about it. I basically knew three things: we loved each other, we were both believers, and we needed to stop living in sin. So, your well-thought questions and concerns are not something I am personally familiar with, although I so admire and appreciate your earnest desire to enter into the covenant of marriage wisely. Honestly, at first, I did not feel qualified to answer your questions, but while I may not have the experience of a beautiful courtship, I do know God was in the midst of our mess, guiding and directing us all the same, and I also have His Word to guide me.

The only criterion the Bible gives believers in looking for a marriage partner is that they be a believer (2 Corinthians 6:14–16). For me to give you a list of things that person needs to be, in addition to having saving faith, would be adding to the Word of God, which I cannot do. However, this doesn't mean the Lord will not give *you* personal standards when looking for a spouse. I want to emphasize that God may very well put on your heart things that He wants you to look for in a future mate, but they would be individual convictions that no one else can give you.

Of course, as a mother, there are things I would very much like my future sons- and daughters-in-law to be before my children marry them (and that I would like my children to be before they get married), but I also know that there were so many things I was not before Mickey married me. He even had apprehensions about marrying me because I was not the easiest person to live with (regrettably, we lived together before marriage). The very unromantic story of our engagement is that we had both just given our lives to Christ and I knew it was wrong for us to be living in sin. When I told him that we needed to get married (I guess you could say I proposed), he responded that he would need two weeks to think about it. *Two weeks!?* So not the answer I was looking for. He had some serious reservations about our frequent fighting, but the Lord led him to marry me anyway. (And I was so thankful it only took about a week for him to decide!)

Even though we had a very rocky beginning, God has done in me, in Mickey, and in our relationship, "far more abundantly than all that we" could have asked or even thought (Ephesians 3:20). I am sharing this to encourage you that our God is in the business of making broken things beautiful. The person He leads you to marry may not be all that you had hoped for, but His plans for us are always best. It is important to remember that everyone marries a sinner, sanctification is a life-long process, and often the things people find difficult about their spouses are used by God to sanctify *them*. Again, please know, I would never encourage anyone to marry someone they had a check in their spirit about. Rather, my heart is to encourage you, my daughters, and any other young women with questions similar to yours, to seek the Lord and trust that He will "direct your paths" (Proverbs 3:5, 6 NKJV)—paths that are for your good and His glory.

You wrote, "I've been pondering what agreement two people need to have in order to be suitable as marriage partners, and I wondered what you have found in your own marriage." I would say that Mickey and I were suitable for each other because we were both believers and were brought together by the Lord. We definitely did not have any agreement other than that, and since being married, have had to work through *many* differences. Some of these areas of disagreement have been ironed out over the years with relatively little incidence; however, there have been other differences that have caused quite a bit of friction. For example, I had no idea how Mickey wanted to raise our future children, but that is probably because we didn't ever even speak about having children. (We were still unsure about getting a fish when we found out we were unexpectedly expecting our first child!) And once we did have them, we had some *very* different views on certain things, which the Lord has been faithful to bring us into unity over (for the most part). The things Mickey leads in that I still feel differently about, I have had to surrender to the Lord.

(Lest anyone think submission has been a piece of cake for me, I need to add that it has definitely *not* been easy letting my husband lead ... which might just be the understatement of the year! But I can also testify that God has been faithful to grow me in this area, and while I am still very much in the growing process, I have been transformed to see, *really see*, the beauty in His design of the roles within marriage. His ways are truly best!)

There have been some things we were in agreement over early on in our marriage (for example, we were "King James Bible Only" for a season) that the Lord has since changed our position on. All of this to say, I believe we are suitable for one another because God brought us together, not because of our agreements (or lack thereof) going into marriage. Of course, God may lead some couples to come to certain agreements before marriage, but they would be personal decisions. Don't forget that our love stories can be as unique as the overall story He writes for our lives.

Much love to you in Jesus,
Laura

Years later, and a bit wiser, I would add this advice to the letter:

P.S. Do not be afraid to seek the prayers and counsel of mature believers as you enter into a relationship with a potential mate. God often uses His people to speak to His people! Just remember, *there is only one Matchmaker.*

Advice is good, but, apart from God's leading, we aren't beholden to it:

I was talked out of carrying a broccoli bouquet in my wedding (yes, the vegetable). The bridesmaids were going to carry asparagus. Looking back, I wish I had just politely insisted that this was what I wanted. (With the right ribbon, it could totally work!)

As you can see, my love story was far from perfect, and my marriage has definitely not been perfect, but it did have the perfect Matchmaker—*God Himself.*

Zeke (3) said, "When you are married, you can kiss every day, right?"

God's Goodness Is a Guarantee

Does this mean that when God brings two people together they are guaranteed a "happily ever after"? No. There is, after all, free will. Some marriages are seriously damaged by sin. Christians sometimes choose to abandon their spouses. People who profess faith in Christ can walk away from Him. But this does not mean that God is not to be trusted. Man may fail us, but *He never will.* Whatever happens to us, He promises to work for our good: "And we know that for those who love God all things work together for good, for those who are called according to his purpose" (Romans 8:28). (I also need to add that God can bring beauty from the ashes of a broken marriage; I have personally seen Him restore a number of marriages and it is so beautiful to see!)

We can also cling to this promise if our Christian child marries an unbeliever. The Bible has encouragement and instructions for those who are unequally yoked in their marriages (1 Corinthians

7:13–16; 1 Peter 3:1, 2), and God will absolutely continue working for good in their lives.

My fellow moms, we can trust the Lord. We can trust Him to lead us from the first moment we hold that precious baby in our arms, to the moment we watch them leave the nest, *and every moment after.* I have not yet done the latter, but I know my God. I know He is faithful and that He is good, no matter what happens. I'd like to end this chapter with a prayer:

Heavenly Father,

Thank You for our children. Thank You for entrusting them to us and blessing us with them. It is a big task, Lord, and we *desperately* need You to guide and strengthen us! Please give us wisdom to direct them while they are children under our care. We also need Your wisdom to counsel them as they face life as an adult.

It is our heartfelt prayer that they will trust in You with all of their hearts and lean not on their own understanding. We pray they will surrender all aspects of their lives to You. May they delight in You; may they be given the desires of their hearts (Psalm 37:4)—*desires that have been aligned with Yours.*

Lord, if it is Your will that they marry, we ask that even now You would be preparing the hearts of their future spouses, and that You would bring them together as You see fit. May they not get ahead of You. If they choose to marry an unbeliever, help us to trust You in that too. Help us to believe that You will work it out for good in their lives, and that Your "hand is not shortened, that it cannot save" (Isaiah 59:1) their unbelieving spouse. (And if our children are not walking with You, may we also never forget that no one is so far that they cannot be reached by Your Spirit.)

Please do in our children's lives above all we could ever ask or imagine, for their good and Your glory. And help us to praise and trust You whether they are exhibiting fruit or not:

> Though the fig tree should not blossom,
> nor fruit be on the vines,
> the produce of the olive fail
> and the fields yield no food,
> the flock be cut off from the fold
> and there be no herd in the stalls,
> yet I will rejoice in the LORD;
> I will take joy in the God of my salvation.
> –Habakkuk 3:17, 18

In Jesus' name,
Amen

---

*A wonderful book on marriage is *When Sinners Say "I Do": Discovering the Power of the Gospel for Marriage.*[37]

*Another great book that looks at marriage through the lens of 1 Corinthians 13 is *Love Without End.*[38]

---

[37] Harvey, Dave. *When Sinners Say "I Do": Discovering the Power of the Gospel for Marriage.* Wapwallopen: Shepherd Press, 2007.
[38] Espinoza, Brooke. *Love Without End.* Bereoa Publishing House, 2003.

Esther Noel Ellis

CHAPTER 13

A Spacious Place

In open fields of wildflowers,
she breathes the air and flies away[39]

In the book *Pilgrim's Progress*, the main character, Christian, struggles along, weighed down by his literal heavy burden of sin. I have a similar picture in my mind regarding my heavy burden of legalism. In my pack was the following: a clock symbolizing the schedules I couldn't follow; a bag of flour representing all the homemade meals I wasn't making for my family on a daily basis; a spray bottle representing the sparkling clean house I thought I was supposed to have; a heavy iron representing the wrinkled clothing I could not seem to stay on top of; a stack of magazines showcasing all the ways my home and I fell short in regard to style; a large textbook for all the times I had failed to teach my children "properly" and had resorted to giving them workbooks instead; and a heavy brick symbolizing the weight of guilt I felt for not cooking, cleaning, clothing, creating, and teaching the way a godly woman was "supposed" to.

In *Pilgrim's Progress*, there is also that awesome point at the cross where Christian's burden tumbles off him. Salvation is being described here, but God wants to do the same with any legalistic burdens we have placed upon ourselves. I wish I could tell you

[39] Haseltine, Dan, Matthew Ryan Bronleewe, Charlie Lowell, and Stephen Daniel Mason. *Jars of Clay*. CD. Franklin: Essential Records, 1995.

that one day I found a particular passage of Scripture, had a mountaintop experience at a retreat, or that God wrote a message for me on the wall and I was suddenly set free from my prison of legalism. Reality is, I am a slow learner and had to learn this lesson over and over *and over again*. The truth had to be presented to me like water rushing over jagged rocks in a riverbed, smoothing them over time. I have had to fall again and again under the crushing weight of legalism in order to begin rejecting it consistently for the easy yoke of Christ. Our ever-patient Savior has gently unpacked my burden, removing the same items countless times.

And He is still unpacking it. As much as I wish I could end this book by declaring that I have been completely set free, the truth is, I am still being set free. But I can attest to the fact that the freedom I have already tasted is glorious! He is bringing me out into a spacious place to love Him and others more fully: "He brought me out into a spacious place; he rescued me because he delighted in me" (Psalm 18:19 NIV). This describes how I feel as the walls of my prison are crumbling. By His grace, I am being ushered into the abundant life of being led by the Spirit to walk in the fruit of the Spirit: "love, joy, peace, patience, kindness, goodness, faithfulness, gentleness, self-control; against such things there is no law" (Galatians 5:22, 23).

My kids once ran around the house singing the hymn "I Need Thee Every Hour," except they had substituted "me" for "Thee."

(How easy it is to forget that we are completely dependent upon the Lord. He not only sets us free—*He alone can keep us free*.)

Transformed by the Renewal of [Our] Mind
–Romans 12:2

And how am I planning to stay free? Besides prayer, Spirit-led reading choices, regular church fellowship, and seeking to take any legalistic thoughts captive and make them obedient to Christ (2 Corinthians 10:5), I need to consistently read the Bible. One of the reasons I became shackled by legalism in the first place was because I didn't really know the Word. I knew what others had to say about it far better than I knew what it had to say for itself. And that grieves me, because daily devotions is something God has put on my heart time and time again to do. The Book, which men like William Tyndale and nameless others gave their very lives for, has often sat neglected on my shelf—as I withered spiritually from lack of its nourishment. Thousands of people have yet to read one word of the Bible in their native tongue, while I have shelved, and subsequently let collect dust, *seven* different English translations over the years. Regrettably, there have been many times when I was much better acquainted with what was going on in the news than I was with what the Lord had for me in His Word, even though I knew He had personally called me to read the Bible far more than He wanted me surfing the web.

No wonder I would get so distressed about bedmaking and dirty windows with such a terrible case of spiritual anemia! God had given me nourishing spiritual food and I kept choosing something else, to my harm. This reminds me of the time I found myself mindlessly munching on a bag of stale popcorn as my family feasted on a delicious dinner my sister had made for us. I suddenly wondered to myself what in the world I was doing eating *that* when such a wonderful meal was available. For *so long*, I needlessly battled the waves of legalism, while God patiently held out the life preserver of His truth, waiting for me to stop thrashing about and go where He had already directed me to go.

Psalm 119:130 says, "The unfolding of your words gives light; it imparts understanding to the simple." (All of Psalm 119 is about the Word—I encourage you to read it.) Those who meditate on God's words day and night will be "like a tree planted by streams of water that yields its fruit in its season, and [whose] leaf does not wither" (Psalm 1:2, 3). His Word is a light on our path as we walk through this dark world (Psalm 119:105). It is: "perfect reviving the soul . . . sure, making wise the simple . . . right, rejoicing the heart . . . pure, enlightening the eyes . . . true, and righteous altogether" (Psalm 19:7–9).

In the same passage, we are told that the Word is more desirable than gold and sweeter than honey. We are warned by it, and there is great reward in keeping God's commands (Psalm 19:10, 11). Moreover, Jesus said that man doesn't live by bread alone, but by every word of God (Matthew 4:4). "All Scripture is breathed out by God and profitable for teaching, for reproof, for correction, and for training in righteousness, that the man of God may be complete, equipped for every good work" (2 Timothy 3:16, 17). We are to "let the word of Christ dwell in [us] richly, teaching and admonishing one another in all wisdom" (Colossians 3:16). "Faith comes from hearing, and hearing through the word of Christ" (Romans 10:17). God has magnified His Word along with His Name: "you have exalted above all things your name and your word" (Psalm 138:2). His Word is "living and active, sharper than any two-edged sword, piercing to the division of soul and of spirit, of joints and of marrow, and discerning the thoughts and intentions of the heart" (Hebrews 4:12). It accomplishes what He purposes, and succeeds in the thing for which He sends it (Isaiah 55:10, 11). His words are spirit and life (John 6:63), and the psalmist wrote, "If your law had not been my delight, I would have perished in my affliction" (Psalm 119:92).

God's Word *Is a Gift!*

The Bible obviously has a lot to say about how important the Bible is! The Lord is clear that we need His Word, sisters, so I encourage you to make it part of your life. It is my prayer that we would never see reading the Bible as a "have to," but that we would see it as a "get to." We get to read God's very words to us, His beloved children. Please know, I am not trying to guilt you into having a time of devotions every day; my heart here is to simply encourage you to read His love letter consistently, because I know how amazing, powerful, and life changing it is. (Of course, reading isn't the only way to make God's Word part of our lives. There are many other ways we can bring Scripture into our busy days. See the following three pages for some ideas.) But I know, I know, *oh, do I know*, it can be hard. Doesn't it sometimes seem that no matter how early you wake up, your kids are not far behind? It is as if they can hear you breathing. Or maybe they can feel the air stirring. I get that. *I live that.* But just because it's hard, doesn't mean we have to throw our hands up or throw our prayer journal away. (See Appendix B for my favorite form of Bible journaling.) We just need to get creative and make the time, as God leads. Think about it: if you have ever planned to watch a movie once the kids were in bed, waited for an "alone moment" to eat the last of the ice cream, or looked forward to some time with your husband once the house was quiet, you know that you made time for it because it was a priority for you. In the same way, busy people often have to make time to meet with God. And even if it is not at a particular time in the day, we can purpose in our hearts to prioritize the reading of His Word. When something is a priority, it is harder to find excuses not to do it.

Excuses, excuses:

*Mickey was sitting with Zeke (~ 3), having a conversation. When Zeke decided to go outside, Mickey said, "But don't you want to talk to me?" Wanting to go, Zeke replied, "I talk too much."

*I asked Elijah (~ 12) if he would like to listen to me practice a teaching I was going to be giving. He thought for a minute (seemingly trying to see how he could get out of it gracefully) and then said, ever so diplomatically, "I can't . . . but get me *the CD!*"

Ways for Busy Moms to Incorporate the Word into Their Days

- Bring your cell phone into the bathroom with you so you can read from any number of Bible apps or online devotionals. (*Daily Light*[40], complied by Samuel Bagster, is a devotional with morning and evening readings, all of which are taken directly out of Scripture. Different verses are arranged together based on themes. You can have it sent directly to your inbox everyday by signing up at https:// www.crosswalk.com/)
- Keep a Bible next to your nursing chair or bed.
- Skip juggling a notebook with your Bible and switch to a Journaling Bible so you can simply jot down notes or prayers as you read.
- Ask the Lord to speak to you as you read to your children from their Bible storybook.
- Get up early and watch the sunrise (or the *sun rise*—as in, higher in the sky—for all of us later risers) as you meet with the Lord (with quite possibly a little person on your lap). My friend Kay kept her children's devotionals next to her bed so she could read to them when they joined her in the morning. Other moms have their kids stay in their bedrooms until a certain time in the morning. You could put a clock in their room and tell them to stay in there (with the exception of an emergency, the need to go to the bathroom, get a drink, etc.) until it reads 7:00 a.m., or whatever time works best for your family.
- Meditate on a passage of Scripture before you go to bed.
- Familiarize yourself with verses that address areas you and your children struggle with.

---

[40] Bagster, Samuel. *Daily Light*. Nashville: Thomas Nelson, 2013.

Wise Words for Moms[41] is a wonderful resource. Designed to hang on your wall, it is an easy Scriptural reference guide for common discipline issues like lying, stealing, and fighting.

- Memorize Scripture with your kids. Coming up with hand motions is fun for them, and also helps with committing the verses to memory.
- Meditate on God's promises to you. There are lots of Bible promise books with verses arranged topically.
- Listen to Scripture songs. (See Appendix C for a list of my favorite CDs.) There was a time I listened to so much Scripture music that I often woke up with the words running through my mind.
- Listen to the Word on CD during a quiet hour in your day. And by "quiet," I know you know that, unless your kids are all sleeping, I am referring to a quieter part of the day.

The Listener's Bible[42] is my favorite Bible audiobook, read by Max McLean.

- *Praise Moves* is an exercise program with postures that are based on Bible verses. It is described as a "Christian alternative to yoga." (The *20-Minute PraiseMoves*[43] DVD is my favorite. Scripture is recited all throughout the workouts!)
- Watch *The Gospel of John*[44], which, in my opinion, is the best Jesus movie ever. (As in, *ever*.) All of the words are taken directly out of the Bible. There was a season in my life when

---

[41] Hubbard, Ginger. *Wise Words for Moms*. Wapwallopen: Shepherd Press, 2001.

[42] Max, McLean. *The Listener's Bible-ESV*. MP3 CD. The Listener's Bible, 2004.

[43] Willis, Laurette. *20-Minute PraiseMoves*. DVD. Eugene: Harvest House Publishers, 2007.

[44] Cusick, Henry Ian and Christopher Plummer. *The Gospel of John*. DVD. Directed by Philip Saville. Toronto: Visual Bible International, Inc., 2003.

I would just leave it playing as I went about my day because it filled my home with God's Word.

* Take a walk and pray the Word! I like to pray for my family with portions of Scripture that I have memorized. For example, the first chapter of Psalms is a great passage to pray over your children: You can ask the Lord to help them not to walk "in the counsel of the wicked, nor [stand] in the way of sinners, nor [sit] in the seat of scoffers." And you can pray that their delight would be "in the law of the Lord" and that they might meditate upon it "day and night."

My mom printed out Scriptures that she wanted to learn on postcard-sized pieces of paper, which she then laminated, punched holes in, and put together on a metal ring. When she goes walking in the morning, she takes them with her to read, meditate upon, and memorize as she walks.

---

* Carry index cards with verses on them in your purse or diaper bag.
* Write Bible verses on your mirrors so you can see them frequently.
* Stencil Scripture on your walls. (Or Sharpie it.)
* If permanent marker or paint sounds too messy, you can also purchase beautiful Scripture decals, or simply hang up photocopies of verses. Years ago, my oldest three kids and I copied Colossians 3:12 and 14 on colored papers (they did one word per sheet, while I wrote out larger portions), and hung them up on a wall (in order, of course). They were up there for about a decade, and the sweet preschool-handwriting became even more precious to me as time went on.

I hope this list didn't overwhelm anyone! Please know, these are *just ideas*. Ask the Lord how He wants you to incorporate His Word into your life—He will lead you.

The Bible is *HIStory*

The more we read the Word, the more reasons we will have to love it; and the more we love it, the more we will probably do it. And here is the best part—the more we do it, the more we can get to know God! As He said to Moses, He is our "exceedingly great reward" (Genesis 15:1 NKJV). My pastor teaches a discipleship class at our church where students learn to study the Word inductively. Inductive Bible Study involves exegesis (the drawing out of the meaning from the text). Many helpful tools can be employed in this process, but one of the most important things he teaches in this class is that whenever approaching the study of the Word of God, we should *first* ask ourselves what the passage tells us about Him. This is referred to as the Theological Lens. God is teaching us about Himself all throughout the Bible!

I believe many legalistic teachings come from Bible study approaches that take God's full character out of the equation, or, in the very least, make it a lesser priority. When we know our God, *really know Him*, we will not be easily misled by legalism:

If He is gentle, will He want us to adopt a method that causes us to be harsh with our children?

If He is patient, will He want us to push our children to perform at a certain level when they just need some more time to grow?

If we know His yoke is easy, will we beat ourselves up for not following something that is practically impossible for us to do?

If we know His burden is light, will we cave to the pressure to take on projects in our home that oppress us and steal our joy?

Knowing God, helps us recognize and say no to legalism. So, let's get to know Him by opening the book He wrote *for us!*

We cannot underestimate the power of the Word to bring clarity to our lives. If you are locked up in the prison of legalism, I encourage you to immerse yourselves in Scripture. Jesus said if we abide in His Word, we will know the truth—and the truth *will* set us free (John 8:31, 32)!

Living a life free from legalism is a gloriously spacious place, sisters! God wants to lead us there. Let us take His hand and follow, for the only place of safety and peace for a mama sheep and her little lambs is in the shadow of the Shepherd:

> He tends his flock like a shepherd:
> He gathers the lambs in his arms
> and carries them close to his heart;
> he gently leads those that have young.
> –Isaiah 40:11 NIV

I'd love to connect with you! You can send me a friend request on my Facebook page @ **Laura Lynn Ellis**

APPENDIX A
The Gospel of Jesus Christ

**There is salvation in no one else,
for there is no other name under heaven
given among men
by which we must be saved.**
–Acts 4:12

The Bible tells us that " 'none is righteous, no, not one; no one understands; no one seeks for God. All have turned aside; together they have become worthless; no one does good, not even one' " (Romans 3:10–12).

There is a popular misconception that if a person is "good enough," meaning they have done enough good deeds to outweigh their bad ones, they will go to heaven. But the Bible tells us differently: "all have sinned and fall short of the glory of God" (Romans 3:23).

This is because God is perfect, holy, and righteous. No one is good enough to stand in His presence, because *all of us* have sinned and fallen short of His glory.

Sin separates us from God: "your iniquities have made a separation between you and your God" (Isaiah 59:2).

When we sin, we are transgressing God's holy laws as found in His Word. Sin deserves punishment: "the wages of sin is death, but the free gift of God is eternal life in Christ Jesus our Lord" (Romans 6:23). This death is also referred to as "the second death"

163

(Revelation 2:11)—it is a complete separation from God in a place of torment called hell.

The Good News!

But the Gospel, which means "good news," tells us that "God shows his love for us in that while we were still sinners, Christ died for us" (Romans 5:8). The blood of Jesus Christ, shed on the cross, washes away the sins of those who place their faith in Him: "In him we have redemption through his blood, the forgiveness of our trespasses, according to the riches of his grace" (Ephesians 1:7).

Some of you may be wondering, Who is Jesus Christ? ("Christ" is His title as God's chosen and anointed One.) Over two thousand years ago, in the land of Israel, Jesus was born in humble circumstances, lived a perfect life, then died on a cross and rose again, victorious over sin and death! Jesus is also called "Immanuel," which means "God with us." Jesus was God incarnate—God in the flesh. You see, only God could live a perfect life, so only He could give His life as payment for the sins of the world.

There is another popular misconception that there are many ways to God, but there is only one Way: Jesus said, " 'I am the way, and the truth, and the life. No one comes to the Father except through me' " (John 14:6). Acts 4:12 tells us that "there is salvation in no one else, for there is no other name under heaven given among men by which we must be saved." Through His death on the cross, we are offered "the free gift of God," which is "eternal life in Christ Jesus our Lord" (Romans 6:23)!

How do we receive this free gift? We acknowledge our sinfulness and need of a Savior. We put our faith in Jesus and turn from pursuing our sinful ways to make Him Lord of our lives: "Repent therefore, and turn back, that your sins may be blotted out" (Acts 3:19); "If you confess with your mouth that Jesus is Lord and believe in your heart that God raised him from the dead, you will be saved. For with the heart one believes and is justified, and with the mouth one confesses and is saved" (Romans 10:9, 10).

In the Jewish temple, there was a thick veil that separated the people from the place that God resided (called "the holy of holies"). When I explained to Eva (6) this was because God is holy and sin cannot be in His presence, she cried out in desperation, "Then who can go to heaven? *Who can go to heaven!?*" How wonderful to be able to tell her that, because of Jesus' death on the cross, the veil was literally torn in two—symbolizing the glorious reality that anyone washed by the blood of Christ and clothed in His righteousness can now enter into the presence of God!

"You Must Be Born Again"
-John 3:7

Jesus explained salvation as being "born again." During the early part of His earthly ministry, He was visited by a religious ruler of the Jews named Nicodemas. In John 3:3–15, we learn the following: Jesus said to him, " 'Truly, truly, I say to you, unless one is born again he cannot see the kingdom of God.' " Nicodemas did not understand how this could be and asked, " 'How can a man be born when he is old? Can he enter a second time into his mother's womb and be born?' " Jesus then explained the rebirth by likening it to the wind that " 'blows where it wishes.' " While we hear the sound of the wind, we do not know where it comes from or where it is going. Jesus went on to say, " 'So it is with everyone who is born of the Spirit.' " Then Nicodemas, referring to the rebirth, asked how these things could be. Jesus told him, " 'As Moses lifted up the serpent in the wilderness, so must the Son of Man be lifted up, that whoever believes in him may have eternal life.' "

Not only are born-again believers saved from the penalty of sin and given eternal life in heaven, we are also saved from the power of sin here on earth. This doesn't mean that Christians never sin—rather, we are no longer slaves to sin, which means we are able, by the power of the indwelling Holy Spirit, to resist temptation and walk in righteousness. He is our Helper—guiding us along the way, giving us spiritual gifts to fulfill our unique purposes in the body of Christ, and enabling us to become more and more like Jesus: "And we all, with unveiled face, beholding the glory of the Lord, are being transformed into the same image from one degree of glory to another. For this comes from the Lord who is the Spirit" (2 Corinthians 3:18).

Zeke (3) made a card for someone, and I was struck by the depth of his simple words when he asked me write: "Jesus loved you on the cross."

"Repent and Believe in the Gospel"
-Mark 1:15

Do you want to be born again?

Do you want eternal life?

Do you believe that Jesus Christ, God incarnate, died on the cross for your sins and rose from the dead?

Do you want to repent of your sins and be cleansed by His blood?

Do you want to turn from following your own way so as to follow Him?

Tell Him. Ask Jesus to be your Savior and Lord, and commit to follow Him all the days of your life. I encourage you to read the Bible, starting with the Gospel of John. I also urge you to find a good Bible-teaching church for regular teaching and fellowship.

Never forget that Christianity is a relationship with the living God! He wants to spend time with you—*so pray often.*

A good website to visit for more information about following Jesus is www.harvest.org.

If anyone is in Christ,
he is a new creation.
The old has passed away;
behold, the new has come.
–2 Corinthians 5:17

*Lulu (6) told me her favorite color was red "because Jesus' blood."

*Esther (4) said, "I believe in Jesus. One day Jesus took my old heart and gave me a new one." (She truly was a new creation from that day on!)

APPENDIX B
A Great Way to Do Devotions

SOAP is a well-known Bible study method. The following explanation has been adapted from one Mickey wrote:

SOAP Journaling

Motivation

Followers of Jesus need to spend time with Him. One way to do this is to follow the simple acronym SOAP, which stands for Scripture, Observation, Application, and Prayer. While definitely not for everyone, journaling is an excellent way to both record and process what God has spoken to us. It is also a useful tool to use at a later time to reflect on and review some of the "gems" that you have received. Without writing them down, you may forget those blessings and some very important lessons that God has taught you.

Preparation

Setting aside a certain time each day helps make devotions a regular part of your life. (*This is not a rule*—it is just a suggestion.) It is also helpful to find a quiet place. This is often not possible for moms, but there are times that are quieter (like the littles' naptime) or less distracting (when your kids are all watching a movie, you are probably less likely to be interrupted). Lastly, pray that the Lord would speak to you from His Word.

Instruction

S is for Scripture: Read through a chapter or section of the Bible. As you read, look for God to direct you to a portion of Scripture to do your devotional study. This may be a few verses, or as small as a portion of one verse. Sometimes you know right away what Scripture He is leading you to; other times, it is less clear, and you may need to reread a few times to find it. When you are done, write out the portion of Scripture next to the letter "S."

Psalm 42:1, 2 (My soul thirsts for God!)

S: "As a deer pants for flowing streams, so pants my soul for you, O God. My soul thirsts for God, for the living God."

O: Theological Lens—Satisfies our need; life-giving
1) The deer's life depends upon finding water.
2) The soul must seek after God as though its life depends upon meeting Him.
3) Streams of fresh water are better and more satisfying than pools of stagnant water.
4) Fresh encounters with God are more satisfying than reliving old encounters.
5) When you drink, you consume water and it actually becomes a part of you.
6) When you meet with God, you receive from Him; His truth becomes a part of you.
7) David is single-minded and steadfast in seeking for God.

A: I need to meet with God regularly as though my life depends upon it.

P: Lord, I have missed three days of devotions, and my soul has been so thirsty. I need You, Lord. Thank You for sustaining me. Thank You for waking me up this morning. Thank You for meeting me in this place. In Jesus' Name, Amen.

O is for Observation: Write down any observations you have concerning the passage. Start with the Theological Lens: what does this tell me about God? Then, begin recording other observations, which might include the context of the passage (the verses surrounding it), points of interest, encouragements, and/or challenges. You might ask regarding the text: Who, What, When, Where, and Why. Do not feel like you *have* to find something profound—the goal here is simply to record what it actually says.

A is for Application: What is the Lord saying to you personally and practically from His Word? Perhaps it is instruction for your day, encouragement for a struggle, revelation of a new promise, or correction for a particular area of your life. Write about how this Scripture applies to *you*.

P is for Prayer: Write down your prayer to God. This can be as simple as asking God to help you use this Scripture or thanking Him for Who He is. It could also be a greater insight on what He may be revealing to you about Himself or His will in your life.

A great Bible Study resource is *How to Study the Bible*[45] by Rose Publishing. It is a pamphlet that explains ten different ways to study the Word.

---

[45] *How to Study the Bible.* Carson: Rose Publishing, Inc., 2009.

APPENDIX C
Scripture Songs

A great way to get the Word into you and your kids is by singing Scripture:

- *Hidden In My Heart* (Volumes I, II and III)
  https://scripture-lullabies.com/
  These are *beautiful* lullaby CDs. Even if you don't have babies anymore, I highly recommend these because they are great for all ages!

- *Hide' Em In Your Heart* (Volumes 1[46] and 2[47])
  While these are "kid songs" (*I know you mamas know what I mean!*), they have become two of my favorite CDs, because hiding dozens of verses in our hearts is definitely worth having my music tastes challenged.

- *SEEDS Worship* (Volumes 1-8)
  http://www.seedsfamilyworship.com/
  This is more mature sounding music that appeals to kids and adults alike.

---

[46] Green, Steve. *Hide 'Em In Your Heart Vol.1*. CD. Brentwood: Sparrow, 2003.
[47] Green, Steve. *Hide 'Em In Your Heart Vol.2*. CD. Brentwood: Sparrow, 2003.

- Sons of Korah
  http://www.sonsofkorah.com/
  They are an Australian band that plays songs with lyrics taken almost exclusively from the Psalms.

- *Glory Revealed* (Volumes I[48] and II[49])
  These CDs are described as "The WORD of GOD in WORSHIP." They are amazing Scripture songs, written and performed by a number of Christian artists—including Third Day and Casting Crowns.

Eva (11) and her friends, Dibora (11) and Bereket (10), were performing a song they had written (that included Scripture) for a couple of us moms. After they had finished singing, and she could see some teary eyes in the room, Dibora said, "I know it works because it makes mamas cry!" Another sister came into the room and they played the song for her too. She also cried, and Dibora exclaimed that they already had "four likes!"

---

[48] *Glory Revealed I.* CD. Brentwood: Reunion, 2007.
[49] *Glory Revealed II.* CD. Brentwood: Reunion, 2009.

Now may the God of peace
who brought again from the dead our Lord Jesus,
the great shepherd of the sheep,
by the blood of the eternal covenant,
equip you with everything good
that you may do his will,
working in us that which is pleasing in his sight,
through Jesus Christ,
to whom be glory forever and ever.
Amen.
–Hebrews 13:20, 21

ACKNOWLEDGMENTS

Many thanks to all those that reviewed my manuscript—*I couldn't have done this without you!* This book would also not have been possible without the support and sacrifice of my family—not only did writing it take a lot of my time, it also cost them much time with me. No one is happier than they are that it is finally *actually* finished!

Printed in the United States
By Bookmasters